air lock

A sacred space
to meet with God

Continuing

D1742095

Welcome to *Airlock*!

Airlock is a Bible-reading guide that contains 13 weeks' worth of undated material. You can use it whenever you like, wherever you like. There are six pages per week – five daily notes and a little extra for the weekend – but feel free to use it in the way that benefits you the most.

Each daily page is divided into three sections:

Decompress

This is a short prayer or thought designed to get you in the right frame of mind to read the Bible, and to prepare you for what you're about to read. After the Decompress section, you'll be given the Bible passage for the day. It doesn't matter what Bible version you use – just make sure you open up your Bible!

Immerse

This section contains ways of relating the Bible passage to today's culture. It also explains anything difficult in the Bible passage, and will help you understand the context the passage was written in.

Re-engage

This section encourages you to take what you've learned from the Bible passage and apply it to your day-to-day life through practical suggestions and pointers.

Contents

Airlock goes systematically through various books of the Bible. This is the third book in the series, although you don't have to read the books in order.

This issue we come to the end of Abraham's story, and continue our voyages through the books of Psalms, Isaiah, Hosea, Obadiah, Matthew, Acts and 1 Corinthians.

Step into the *Airlock* and relieve the pressure!

Written by Jenny Baker (C/31–35), Andy Brown (C/11–15), Simon Hall (C/56–60), Darren Hill (C/61–65), Howard Ingham (C/26–30), Carsten Lorenz (C/21–25), James Lovelock (C/16–20), Andy Perry (C/36–40), Chris Pope (C/41–45), Al Rodgers (C/06–10), Steve Tilley (C/46–50), Steve Tomkins (C/51–55) and Dave Walker (C/01–05).

Edited by Andrew Cupples, Lizzie Green and Darren Hill.

Designed and illustrated by Martin Lore. Cover photography by Chris Brown.

Printed and bound in Great Britain by Maston Digital, Didcot, Oxon

Extreme soap opera

C/01

Decompress

What has made you into the person you are today? Think of the different influences on your life – your upbringing, friends, what you watch, read, your culture etc.

Now read Genesis 19:30–38

Immerse

Despite their best efforts, even the greatest soap operas of today haven't come up with a story this depraved. The two daughters of Lot have sex with their father and get pregnant in order to continue the family line.

>But why? It's unthinkable… isn't it? Or is it, when you realise that they had grown up in the city of Sodom? Maybe they'd have acted differently if they could have seen into the future – the descendants of the two daughters became the Moabites and the Ammonites who would cause massive problems as enemies of Abraham's descendants. (See 1 Samuel 14:47)

>How often do people act differently when others influence them? However, this goes a bit deeper than just going along with the crowd. For one thing Lot and his daughters were alone. They were influenced by both the situation –

they weren't married and therefore weren't going to be having any children in a culture which attached significant importance to the continuance of the family line; and by the fact that they'd been brought up in a very dodgy society

>Lot's daughters chose to go along with the way of life they had experienced growing up in Sodom. What are some of the influences on us? Are we aware that not all of them will be in line with the way God might want us to live?

Re-engage

Identify one influence on your life that is having a negative effect. Make a plan to combat it, either by removing it from your life, eg not watching a certain TV programme, or by standing up against it, eg telling your friends about what you believe in. However, in all of the above, take it to God in prayer first.

>And one further difficult question for you to think about – how can we be aware of the influences on us without isolating ourselves from the outside world?

White lies? Don't do it!

C/02

Decompress

'Lord, it is so easy to forget that you are with me always! Please prompt me when I face a challenge and forget your promises.'

Now read Genesis 20:1-10

Immerse

Does the stupidity of people in soap operas ever wind you up? It seems that even the characters we like the most do the stupidest of things from time to time. It also seems stupidity isn't limited to the characters that are there for the light comic relief.

>And what about our own lives? How many times have we walked away from a situation, metaphorically holding our head in our hands, and asking 'Why on earth did I do that?'

>Abraham is one of the big 'heroes' of the Old Testament, but in today's passage he doesn't show it at all. Abraham and Sarah had been promised a child back in chapter 18. But when they moved into a new neighbourhood, they seemed to forget this promise, and self-preservation became the highest priority for them. Abraham was so afraid that Abimelech would kill him and take Sarah that he told the king that his wife was, in fact, his sister.

>This 'white lie' was a deception he had used before, way back in chapter 12. But just like back then, when things went completely pear-shaped and people got horrible diseases as a result, things went wrong again. This time Abimelech came and took Sarah away. Fortunately God intervened. If only Abraham had held onto God's promises in the first place... What has God promised those who follow him?

Re-engage

From now on, think before you speak. It's astonishing how easy it is to put your mouth into action without engaging your brain, but it can lead to disaster, as Abraham found out.

>Also, take note today of how many times people ask you a question and you reply in a way that is not exactly true. This is especially true in church when people ask, 'How are you?' or 'Is everything OK?' – let your yes, be yes and your no be no. If you're having a rough time, then tell them.

Airlock: Continuing

The Power of reconciliation

C/03

Decompress

'Lord, let me be the bringer of calm and reconciliation to disputes and hurt. Guide me to sort things out rather than create more of a mess.'

Now read Genesis 20:11–18

Background

Verse 12 says that Sarah was Abraham's half-sister. This meant that Terah was her father, but she had a different mother to Abraham.

>Verse 16 says that 1,000 pieces of silver were given. At the time when these events took place, there was no system of coinage available. All gold and silver transactions were based on weight until about the 7th Century BC. These events took place in approximately 2000 BC.

Immerse

How often do you hear someone offering an excuse for something that they've done wrong?

'It wasn't my fault because...'
'I wasn't the one who...'
'I didn't do that...'
'Someone else made me...'

>A more worrying situation is when we hear ourselves talking like this – and it's an easy trap to fall into

>Abraham tries to wriggle out of the situation on a technicality. But the fact was, he'd been deceitful in order to attempt to get his way. Reconciliation occurs as the two men make their peace. The king takes the lead and offers gifts, while Abraham in turn prays for Abimelech.

>Abimelech took the lead in patching things up, even though the situation was only partly his fault. Sometimes we need to do the same – even if we're the ones who feel we have been wronged.

Re-engage

Is there someone who you are in disagreement with? Take the lead in sorting it out, even if the situation wasn't 'your fault'. If necessary, consider asking someone else, maybe someone older and wiser, to act as a third party – to offer advice and to make suggestions.

>Another one of those difficult questions for you – is it right to say sorry for something that's not your fault, for the sake of patching things up? Why?

You've got to laugh

Decompress

Who are the funniest people you know? What makes you laugh? Is there anything about your faith that makes you laugh regularly? Or should religion and humour be completely separate?

Now read Genesis 21:1–7

Immerse

As a cartoonist, I spend a certain amount of time thinking of ways to make people laugh. One of the highly secret secrets of cartooning, or in fact any humour, is that people laugh at the unexpected. I was in a highly serious meeting the other day when a workman walked past the window pushing a wheelbarrow. There's nothing funny about workmen or even wheelbarrows in themselves, but because it was unexpected I found it highly amusing. Err… I guess you had to be there....

>In chapter 18, Sarah had laughed at the suggestion she was about to have a child, but when asked why she had laughed, she denied it. She was laughing at the unexpected – but her laughter revealed her lack of faith.

>Now, when it all happens just as God said it would, she finds herself laughing again. This time she says, 'Everyone who hears about this will laugh with me.' Once again Sarah laughed at the unexpected, but this time it was joyful laughter. God's promise had come true.

>And the relevance of all this laughter? Well, the name Isaac literally means, 'he laughs'.

Re-engage

God did the unexpected. Abraham was very old, as was Sarah, and without going into the medical details, it was pretty unlikely that they were going to have a baby. And yet in walks God and, well… you know the story.

>God is in the business of doing the unexpected, from the big – becoming one of us – to the small – gifting Sarah with a son. Although you can't really say that size matters with God, because they are amazing things, and he's still doing amazing things today.

>Spend some time in prayer asking God to do the unexpected in your life, so that you can serve him and do his will.

Airlock: Continuing

In the desert

C/05

Decompress

Think of a time in your life when things seemed hopeless. How did you feel? If you feel that way now, ask God to speak to you through his word.

Now read Genesis 21:8–21

Immerse

Hagar goes through a really rough time in today's passage. Sent away from everyone and everything she had known, sent into the desert with just a bag of water and a bit of food, the situation was looking pretty bleak for her and Ishmael. Their water supply quickly became exhausted, and it looked like the end.

>But it wasn't.

>Likewise, we all go through really difficult times in life, both spiritual and physical struggles. When we're going through a difficult patch, when life is tough and joy seems a thing of the distant past, when we're in a complete spiritual desert and all around is emptiness, it can look like the end...

>But it isn't for us either.

Re-engage

It would be easy for me to write 'If you're going through a desert experience, God will sort everything out in the very near future, and it will all end happily, just as it did for Hagar and Ishmael.' But unfortunately, life isn't that simple.

>But what I can say is that if you're at a low point, this *isn't* the end. Things *will* get better. Talk to God, talk to a friend, keep on going. Keep on trusting in him. If you're having difficulty seeing God in the present, look back to a time when he was clearly with you and draw strength from that.

>Perhaps you know of someone else who is going through a desert experience at the moment? What could you do to encourage them? Pray with them, and for them. Make sure they know that you're there for them. What other practical ways could you help them to get beyond their troubles?

>PS Check out Galatians 4:21–31 where Paul talks about Isaac and Ishmael in an encouraging and uplifting way.

Airlock: Continuing

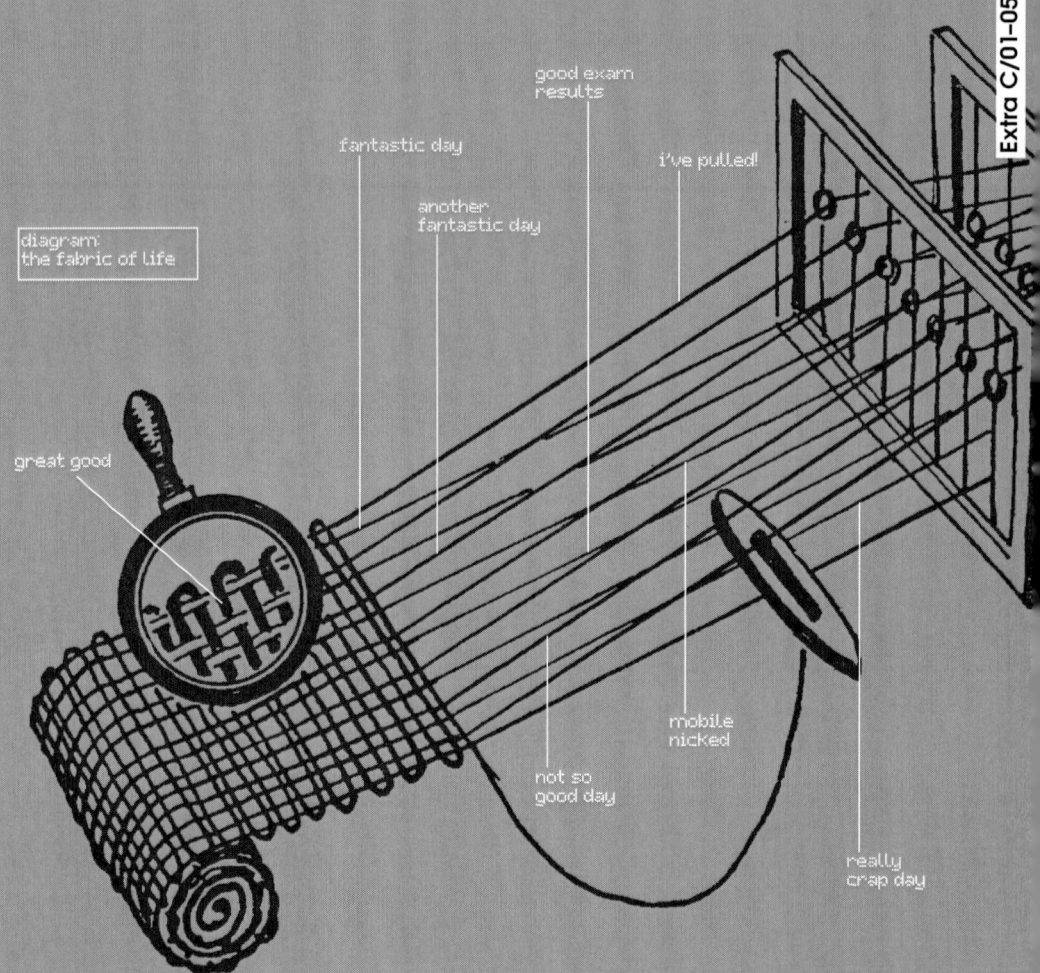

diagram:
the fabric of life

good exam
results

fantastic day

another
fantastic day

i've pulled!

great good

mobile
nicked

not so
good day

really
crap day

'We know that in everything God
works for the good of those who
love him. They are the people he
called, because that was his plan.'
Romans 8:28

Is Romans 8:28 something we say to
make us feel good when we are
feeling down, or is it a promise that
we need to hold on to, despite what
is going on in our lives? Why?

Extra_1 Romans 8:18–30
Extra_2 Romans 8:31–39

Themes: Scary stuff, trust

Scary movie?

C/06

Decompress

OK. So it's not cool to be scared, but most people are rattled by something. What scares you most? Are you scared of anything today?

Now read Isaiah 8:11-15

Immerse

Even if people don't like to admit it, they are scared of stuff. Terrorism. Crime (a kid got murdered down the road from me recently). Money (not having enough). Loneliness (having too much). Death. Life. Illness. Flying. Spiders. Velcro (yes – it really happens). The dark. Birds. Some of it we can understand. Some of it we can't.

>Isaiah probably wouldn't have been called a lightweight if he was scared. He showed up about the time that King Uzziah of Judah died, which was the end of fifty years of peace. After that, four neighbouring countries (who had kings with great names – Tiglath-Pileser III, Shalmaneser II, Sargon II & Sennacherib) turned out not to be good friends, with their plans to take over the world. This included wanting to take over Israel and Judah, the 'two families of Israel' (God's chosen people who'd split into two by then).

>In their panic, the people around Isaiah were looking for anything to hold on to, or any country to team up with, as they tried to not be the next victim of their power-crazy neighbours.

Re-engage

When life gets scary, it's easy to look for someone else to blame, or to look for stuff to protect us. But here's Isaiah in as scary a situation as most of us will ever face. And he says it's God that people should be worried about. Not the countries next door that look like they might flatten them.

>God can be a 'rock' that we use as protection and a solid foundation ('...he will be a place of safety for you.') or he can be a 'rock' we trip over as we try to find someone, or something else to be our bullet-proof vest. Of course there's nothing wrong with doing sensible stuff to be safe. A bullet-proof vest in a war zone is a good idea. But it's when we start to trust other stuff instead of God that things go wrong.

>Stop. Think. Pray. Is there anything that you're trusting more than God? Is there anything you need to do to shift that trust?

Airlock: Continuing

Signs

Decompress

How do you feel about 'the future'? How much do you feel God is in control of it? How much do you want to know about it now?

Now read Isaiah 8:16–22

Immerse

Horoscopes, tarot cards, psychic shows on TV – people want to know the future before they get there. We could argue about whether all these things 'work', but that's not the point. God says they are bad (eg, in Deuteronomy 18:9–13), and here he tells us why – because they don't tell you what God thinks, they don't 'speak the word of the Lord'. Why would anyone want to hear what dead people think, when they can hear the truth from the real God who is alive and knows?

>Isaiah was a prophet, but that didn't make his main job telling the future. There were loads of people who said they could do that (and probably made good money from it), but Isaiah's job was to be like a text message from God, giving God's perspective on the way his people were living their lives. Sometimes that meant talking about the future, but often it meant talking about now – and being unpopular, telling people they'd lost God's plot.

Airlock: Continuing

Re-engage

In verses 16 to 18, Isaiah tells us about a choice we all still have. We can wait for God, even if that means being part of a very small group hanging on for him (like Isaiah); or we can stop trusting God and try to short circuit the future, either by trying to download a trailer for our lives through stuff the Bible tells is dodgy, or (like Isaiah 8:11–15 was saying) by getting such a tight handle on our own future (and our ambitions, dreams and careers) that there's no room left for God.

>Waiting for God might be long, tiring and even scary. Trying to second guess the future might look instant and exciting. But Isaiah knew which way was best.

>Who holds your future? You? Fate? Other people? God? You and God working together? Why not take a piece of paper and write down your big hopes. Then ask God to take his plans for you, work with you on them, and redesign any of your selfish plans? Keep the piece of paper somewhere safe and look at it in a year. You might be amazed, when you look back, to see how God has answered your prayer.

Mission impossible

C/08

Decompress

Do you feel like God has given you an impossible dream? Have you seen the end of the story yet? Have you asked God about it recently? Would now be a good time?

Now read Isaiah 9:1-7

Immerse

God is into making the impossible possible. If he wasn't, we wouldn't be sitting here on a planet which is so amazingly designed that a slight change in the speed the planet spins, or a slight change in the recipe of the atmosphere, would make life impossible. And that's just a start. We wouldn't be reading the greatest love story ever between God and his creation either, or talking about it to our mates, or singing about it in church. And we wouldn't be talking about Jesus being alive, because unless God was into the impossible, Jesus would just be a name on a tombstone.

>God is into the impossible, and the impossible is exactly what Isaiah was talking about here.

Re-engage

In the middle of a country that looked very much like it was going to be destroyed, Isaiah suddenly starts talking about a peaceful future where the country would be strong and grow and the people would be happy. And it wasn't going to come through some powerful King in a palace, but through a baby boy being born.

>It sounds like something out the Christmas story, and that's because it is – it wasn't going to happen over night. Jesus (seven hundred years later) was part of God's big plan that Isaiah was talking about.

>It was all an impossible dream, until God made it possible in a way that nobody expected. And God wasn't just the God of impossible dreams two or three thousand years ago. He's still at it now.

>Go back to your impossible dreams. Are you ready for God to surprise you and work at them in the last way you might expect?

>Pray, thanking God for the impossible dreams you've seen him work out. Pray for people you know who need the impossible now. Pray for your impossible dreams that you're still waiting for God's action in.

Airlock: Continuing

Comfort zones

C/09

'But you are a chosen people, royal priests, a holy nation, a people for God's own possession. You were chosen to tell about the wonderful acts of God, who called you out of darkness into his wonderful light.'
1 Peter 2:9

>How does it feel to be chosen by God today?

Now read Isaiah 9:8–17

Immerse

We live in a culture where an amazing lifestyle is one of the BIG aims. Just watch the adverts on TV – the endless quest for the most comfortable, stress-free, hassle-free, dirt-free, bacteria-free, wait-free, calorie-free, exercise-free lifestyle is big dollar. And it's easy to believe the adverts – because we have all this stuff stacked round us – good health care, big chunky cars, insurance policies – it's easy to think that nothing can touch us. We're invincible.

>And we're not the first people to think it. Take a look at verse 10. Isaiah was bringing God's message to people who thought they would last forever. Not because of all the stuff they owned, but because they were God's chosen people. If God was on their side (they thought), who could touch them?

Airlock: Continuing

Re-engage

It's great to be chosen, but if it means we spend all our time being proud that we've been chosen, instead of getting on with the responsibility of being God's representatives, then we might leave God behind.

>And that's exactly what happened with Israel. They'd started off on God's side, but they hadn't kept up with God. It wasn't just the leaders that got it wrong either – take a look at verses 16 and 17. The ordinary people – including young people, orphans and widows – were in the dock too. They were so chuffed and confident that they were God's chosen people that they missed the point. And God was using Israel's power-crazy neighbours as a wake-up call. Ouch.

>Do we need a wake up call? Are we living out the responsibilities God has given us, or are we sitting back and enjoying the view as God's chosen people?

>Look at what you did last week. Did being one of God's chosen people change anything about your week? Look at next week. Should being one of God's chosen people change anything about your week?

Bush fires

Decompress

Do you have any 'no-go-zone' relationships? People you really can't cope being with? People you cross the street to avoid? Pray for them. Ask God to help them. Ask God to help you see them in the same way that he does.

Now read Isaiah 9:18 –10:4

Immerse

Recently a huge fire in Colorado burned 137,000 acres of forest, levelled 133 houses and cost $39 million to put out. Expensive, sad, even a disaster maybe. But weird too. Because a Forest Service employee was accused of starting the fire herself. And it all started when she tried to burn a letter from her husband. Isaiah was right. Fire can travel fast.

>And not just fire, but evil too. It's all in this bit of Isaiah. Selfishness, cannibalism, civil war, unfair laws and exploitation... all from God's chosen people.

>But the passage is about more than just relationships between individuals. It's about a whole country and it's about disaster starting small. If Israel as a country was full of people who had good relationships with each other, things could never have gone so wrong. But instead Isaiah was bringing God's warning about bad relationships spiralling out of control into an 'every person for themselves' type survival attitude. Not only were God's chosen people being attacked from outside, but the bits of their country they could have been most proud of were in danger of ripping themselves apart too.

Re-engage

Things can go horribly wrong, and it can start very small – unsorted relationships which get out of hand and blow up into World War 3; small lies which get covered with bigger and bigger lies; ignoring small injustices because life's too short.

>And it's very easy to look at other people and see where they're going wrong. But sometimes God asks us to look at ourselves, and our own churches. Are there 'fires' we need to take a look at before they get out of hand? Are there 'fires' that have already started to spread? Is there anything that you can do about them?

>If you're need to do some fire control, try talking to someone you trust who's outside the situation. Pray with them to get God's help. It might help get a more balanced perspective. Do you need to say sorry to anyone, or rebuild any relationships?

Airlock: Continuing

Warning:

Reading the Bible can seriously affect your life.

Do not read while driving, or while operating heavy machinery. If used incorrectly, may cause drowsiness.

Isaiah isn't the only part of the Bible that talks about evil spreading like fire. James 3:1–12 should carry a health warning, because it's dangerous stuff if you want an easy and unchallenged life.

Extra_1 James 3:1–12
Extra_2 James 3:13–18

Cost, faith and healing

C/11

Decompress

'Lord, just as I put you first in this time spent reading your word, Help me put you first in every part of my life!'

Now read Matthew 8:18–22

Immerse

It's Sunday morning, the bed is warm, the house is warm and breakfast is waiting to be cooked. It's cold outside, but it's time for church – that cold dark building. Hmmmm. WWID? What would I do?

>It's Wednesday evening, cheap night at the cinema, and you're getting ready to go with your cool friends. The phone rings and it's your youth leader. One of the guys from youth group is ill and your group is having an emergency prayer meeting for him. Hmmmm. WWID? What would I do?

>This should be a really challenging passage for us as Christians. Basically, if we are serious about following Jesus, nothing else should matter. We could be asked to go anywhere, we may never have comfort or security (in a worldly sense), and we have to put everything, even the death of a loved one, after what we believe. What are you willing to give up for him?

Re-engage

If you look back at the first few years of Jesus' life, he was basically a nomad, a refugee. He was born in Bethlehem, then was taken to Egypt for fear of death, then went to Israel, then finally to Nazareth. And the latter part of his life, once he started his ministry, was spent totally on the road. This is another challenge for us. He didn't have a nice house, home comforts, a regular income, a fast car. He had nothing and relied on God for everything. This is a warning to his followers that they will have to do the same.

>What's our response to this? Well, we need to look at our priorities in life. What do we hold dear? What would we be willing to give up if God asked us to? Where would we be willing to go if he asked us? Where wouldn't we be willing to go?

>Write down the ten most important things in your life in order. If God isn't at the top, ask yourself if you are willing to rearrange things to put him there. If he is, cross off some of the things you know you could lose, and then go even further and see how many things other than him you'd be willing to let go of. Then PRAY!

Airlock: Continuing

Faith, cost and healing

C/12

Decompress

Have you ever thought you were going to die? I've come close on a couple of occasions, but the disciples here were sure this was the last boat trip they'd ever take. Think *Titanic*. Think *Perfect Storm*. Think *White Squall*. Think *Twister* (and add water!). This was a seriously big storm – 'the waves covered the boat'. Just take a minute to put yourself in that situation.

Now read Matthew 8:23–27

Immerse

I reckon the closest I've come to death was when I was living in Australia. I got into bodyboarding and a couple of times I went for waves that were far too big. The power of the water is incredible and I'd get swept clean out of the sea up into the air, then the next moment I'd be getting dragged along the bottom. There were a few times when I'd breathed out all the air in my lungs, I didn't know which way was up, and the current was holding me under. It was pretty scary. I think the only word that ever comes to mind in those situations is HELP! And that was the same for the disciples here.

Re-engage

I have really started to notice recently that I'm growing stronger in my faith. I give every day to God. I know that he has a plan for me and he will provide and look after me. Matthew 8:18–22 was about the cost of following Jesus and what we have to give up. Well, there's no way we can drop everything for someone we don't have faith in.

>Think about times when you are most likely to panic and worry. What are you scared of 'drowning' in? School? Family? The future? We don't always get immediate answers from God, and we don't always get the answers we want. But our faith and trust in him makes a huge difference. Starting a difficult day knowing that you have given it all to God and told him that you rely on him to get you through does make a difference, I promise you! So start now – give all you have to God and rely on him. If you look up reliable in the dictionary, it says 'God'. Well, OK, it doesn't, but perhaps it should...

Airlock: Continuing

Cost, faith and healing

C/13

Decompress

Sometimes I think (and I'm sure I'm not the only one) that if only Jesus were here now to perform some miracles or heal some people, then everyone would believe in him. But actually when I read passages like this, I'm not so sure. There were actually plenty of people around then who saw all the evidence, but chose not to believe in him.

Now read Matthew 8:28–34

Immerse

Jesus comes into this village and heals the two demon possessed men, which does not only them a favour, but everyone else as well. They were 'so dangerous that people could not use the road'. We don't know how the guys themselves reacted, but look at what the people in the village did – 'they begged him to leave their area'.

>Why? Well, I think for two reasons. One – they were scared, both of Jesus' power, and probably at the sight of these mental pigs all committing suicide. Not something the average farmer sees on a daily basis. But more importantly, the people were probably more concerned about their financial loss than the deliverance of the demon-possessed men. Isn't that sad?

Re-engage

We've already looked at the cost of following Jesus. And here we can see a clear example of people turning him away because the cost is too high. The price of a few dead pigs was more important than the healing of two sick men, and a man who had the power to do it. Don't let the cost of following him put you off. Yes, we need to seriously consider the cost and not follow him blindly, but don't be so overcome by the price-tag that you reject the gift.

>Are you limiting God's power in your life by counting the cost? Look at how you react to situations today. Is your first thought about how you can show God in this event or how you will look?

>Spend some time praying that God will be your first thought in everything you say and do.

Airlock: Continuing

Cost, faith and healing

C/14

Decompress

I do struggle sometimes with the issue of healing. In New Testament times it seemed to happen so often, but now I know so many people who could really do with healing, and they don't get it. A family from our church recently lost a father who died of a recurring brain tumour. They thought it had gone away but it came back. Another mother died a few years ago of MS, she just wasted away. And now another mum of three kids has got it too. If God has the power to heal, why doesn't he?

Now read Matthew 9:1–8

Immerse

The critic might look at this passage and say; well Jesus only healed people a few times to prove he was who he claimed to be. He only needed to do it when he was alive, and there's no need for healing to happen now. Plus he was in his own town so he wanted to make a good impression. But I don't think these are the real issues.

>Firstly, and we've already looked at this in this series, there's the issue of faith. Look at verse 2. Now in those days they didn't have wheelchairs or those ambulance stretchers with wheels on them.

They didn't have nice easy roads to walk on. And wherever Jesus went there was always a massive crowd, so getting this disabled guy to the feet of Jesus would have been big effort. He saw their faith.

>I can't make a statement like 'people don't get healed these days because those who pray for them don't have enough faith' because there is no way of knowing that. But for me, when I look at the faith that some people in the Bible had, I really wish I was like them. And God rewards faith. I wonder what my relationship with him would be like if I had their faith. Secondly (and more importantly) Jesus' first move ISN'T to heal the man. He forgives him. And that's the key. Being forgiven is much more important than being healed.

Re-engage

Next time you think God's being unfair, either because someone's still ill or hurt, or for any other reason, remember that he invented fair. He is more than fair because none of us deserve to have our sins forgiven but he forgives us. He's so fair he sent his own son to die for us.

>Have one of those great thankful prayer times – praise God out loud.

Airlock: Continuing

Cost, faith and healing

C/15

Decompress

'Dear Lord, show me what the words "follow me" really mean; how they should impact the way I think, the words I say and the things I do.'

Now read Matthew 9:9-13

Immerse

This passage is a culmination of cost and faith. There really is a literal cost here. The passage doesn't say: 'Matthew finished doing his paperwork, packed up his drawers, emptied his filing cabinet, wrote a letter of resignation to the central Capernaum Tax Office, deposited the tax into the building society and put a 'closed until further notice' sign up on the booth.'

>He just got up and followed Jesus. Imagine what his employer thought! Anyone wanting to make a quick buck could have raided the stall, taken the cash and got access to all his financial details. It's not that Matthew was an irresponsible worker; he just knew it was time to leave.

Re-engage

Within hours Matthew was reaping the rewards of his faith and sacrifice. Tax collectors were mainly seen as the bad guys because they charged people too much and kept the extra for themselves. So even if he was a good tax collector (we don't really know), people would still have tarred him with the same brush. But hours after controversially quitting his job on the spot, this man who reckoned he was the Son of God is round at Matthew's house having tea. His faith in Jesus brings him into God's family and God's love; Jesus gives him value and respect, and puts the Pharisees into their place for good measure.

>Who do you know that needs to give up their lifestyle and follow Jesus? In some ways, this may be you. I can't imagine throwing down literally EVERYTHING to follow him, and we may not ever be asked to do exactly that, but the key issue is that we need to be willing to do it. Abraham was willing to kill Isaac just because God said so, but he didn't end up having to do it.

Airlock: Continuing

What have I learned about faith
and cost over the last few days?

Would I be willing to give up
everything to follow Jesus?

How much of a difference would
it make if he was here and asked
me himself?

Extra_1 Romans 4:1-12
Extra_2 Corinthians 4:13-18

That's what I call worship

C/16

Decompress

'...I am happy when I have weaknesses, insults, hard times, sufferings and all kinds of trouble for Christ. Because when I am weak, then I am truly strong' (2 Corinthians 12:9,10).

Now read Psalm 16

Immerse

This is one of the most positive of the Psalms – David was obviously having a good day! I really like the way that David prays his simple prayer in verse 1: 'protect me God, because I trust in you'. The rest of the psalm is an outpouring of David's trust – if you like, a rough working of David's argument for trusting the Lord.

>David specifically praises God for 'godly people' in verse 3. Alas, the idea of 'godliness' for me has the unfortunate effect of conjuring up a Pharisee wagging his finger about how ungodly I am. But it is certainly not wrong to praise God for those people in which Jesus is so clearly seen – these are the true godly ones!

Re-engage

So what are we supposed to do with these psalms then? Find a two thousand year old tune and sing it every week in church? Modernise the words and delete all the bits that are not relevant and sing it to the tune of 'Lady in Red' complete with actions? Pray the whole thing as a monotone prayer in between the bible reading and praying for the PCC secretary's ingrowing toenail?

>Actually, David and the other psalm-writers used these poems, songs and prayers for their personal worship to God. They praised him, thanked him, shouted at him, pleaded with him and cried to him. They didn't worry whether their choice of words would meet with people's approval, or whether their tune was good enough to get on 'Now That's What I Call Worship'. They just 'sang their hearts out' – literally praying everything out to God. Now that's what I call worship!

>'Protect me, God, because I trust in you.' What is your argument for trusting God? Try writing it out – you never know, you might end up with your own psalm to God!

>Think about your attitude to worship songs in church. Are there things that you need to change about the way you approach your church service?

Airlock: Continuing

A cure for inferiority complexes

Decompress

'But to all who did accept him and believe in him he gave the right to become children of God' (John 1:12).

Now read Psalm 17

Immerse

I am quite clear about the fact that I am not King David. This is fortunate, really, as dancing nudily around the church and marrying lots of different women would probably get me arrested. But looking at this psalm (and many of the others) can give a Christian a really bad inferiority complex! If David is speaking the truth in the first six verses (and the fact that it's in the Bible suggests he is), then we've got a lot to live up to. Thanks to God, we can say the same thing, through Jesus. And we must always remember that the sacrifice of Jesus was made so that we have a clear way to God without obstacles. We would be very ungrateful not to use it!

Re-engage

David sets out the message of his prayer in verse 7 – God's wonderful love will save those who trust him from their enemies. This is the important bit for us to get hold of today – if God is on our side we are unbeatable! Later in verse 14, David reminds us that material prosperity is not necessarily a sign of God's favour. Sometimes we get caught up in a jealous crusade against non-Christians who are particularly wealthy and we forget that this is really not an issue for God. He is more interested in looking after those without food and shelter than getting hot and bothered about people with wealth!

>And if you're still tempted by the material wealth, then read verse 15 – 'because I have lived right, I will see your face. When I wake up, I will see your likeness and be satisfied'. I don't think we can ask much more than that, really...

>Often in our conflicts, right and wrong are not quite as clear as in David's case. Read Romans 12:9–21, and think about how you can successfully deal with your enemies without the need to persecute them.

Righteous anger

C/18

Decompress

'...in Christ, he chose us before the world was made so that we would be his holy people – people without blame before him' Ephesians 1:4.

Now read Psalm 18:1–19

Immerse

At the age of 15, I was painfully shy around other kids, particularly with new people. So it was a bit of a surprise to find myself at a youth camp with my uncle's church, with 40 teenagers who I didn't know.

>One night, the leader asked at the evening meeting if anyone wanted to come to the front for prayer. I found myself stumbling forward, eager to find anything that could make me feel more secure about myself. As the leaders prayed for me, I had a strange experience, almost like fainting, and I had a vision – a panoramic view of the outside of a castle, and I heard a voice saying 'I am God'. And then I saw a small, empty room, and I knew it was prepared for me.

>And I wonder – did God tear open the sky and ride his winged creature on the wings of the wind that night to reach me in that one safe place just because he delights in me?

Airlock: Continuing

Re-engage

This passage is more than just God showing off about how awesome he is when he gets cross! The whole key to the passage is verses 16 to 19 – the root of God's anger is that he delights in his people (v 19) and he cannot bear to see them suffering. Think about the emotions you feel when you see someone you love suffering – because these emotions are exactly how God feels, and it's no wonder he sometimes gets angry! And often all he is waiting for is a cry for help (v 6) before he leaps into action, scatters the enemy and protects the children that he loves.

>So many people are struggling with the ropes of death and the deadly rivers in their lives, but so few think to call to God for their help. Pray for some of the people that you know are hurting at the moment – that they would allow God to release his righteous anger to scatter their enemies and pull them from the water!

>Testimonies can be a powerful witness to God continuing his work in the world today. When has God unleashed his power to save you from your enemies? Are you still swimming out of your depth and in need of a safe place? Call to the Lord and he will save you!

Living in mysterious ways

C/19

Decompress

Show me your ways, O Lord,
Teach me your paths,
Guide me in your truth and teach
me,
For you are God my saviour,
And my hope is in you all day long
(Psalm 25:4,5).

Now read Psalm 18:20–36

Immerse

I'm sure you've heard or used the
phrase 'God works in mysterious
ways' before – the convenient little
phrase that covers up all the little
theological knots and the spiritual
holes that we get ourselves into.

>Well, God's got news for you.
Yes, his ways are mysterious, but
not impossible for us to follow – in
fact, learning to follow in God's
ways is our entire purpose on this
planet!

>This is another one of those
situations where you just want to
mumble the first seven verses of the
passage and then get to the nice
safe bit. I don't know about you,
but I don't always feel that I
remember all God's laws, follow his
ways and keep myself from doing
evil (v 22,23). Perhaps an area for
development and prayer? And
quite a few 'thank-you Gods' for
sending Jesus, I should imagine.

>Also beware of the warning of
verse 27 – pride is so often a
sticking point in our relationship
with God. Why is it that despite the
fact that God's ways always work,
we have to try our own way first? I
think that pride has a lot to answer
for!

>Look at the promises in verses
28–35, summed up in verse 36. The
idea of trusting God for protection
is important again here – just look
at all those benefits! I particularly
love that bit in verse 35, 'you have
stooped to make me great'. He
really cares about us, you know!

Re-engage

Over the next few days, take stock
of some situations in your life where
you could do with following God's
ways. If you're stuck about what
God's ways are, why not ask an
older friend – they've got a lot
more experience of God!

>How can we find out more
about the ways of God? Do you
think that it is really possible to live
your whole life following God's
ways? How can this be achieved?

Airlock: Continuing

The blessed ones

C/20

Decompress

'You have heard that it was said, "Love your neighbour and hate your enemies." But I say to you, love your enemies. Pray for those who hurt you. If you do this, you will be true children of your Father in heaven' (Matthew 5:43–45).

Now read Psalm 18:37–50

Immerse

So picture the scene. You've followed this huge crowd up a very tall mountain – and they're saying that the one they are following will be the new King, a descendant of David and Solomon and all the other great warrior-kings from Scripture – the one that David predicted would set the Jews free. Will he turn the Romans to rivers of mud and stomp all over them singing 'We are marching in the light of god'? And what is the rallying cry, the victory chant of this new King?

>'Blessed are the peacemakers for they will be called sons of God.'

>You what? After all those battles and all the fantastic war victories? And after all those promises to destroy our enemies? Surely not. We must have misheard. Maybe the cheesemakers are in for a good spell after all...

Re-engage

David seems to be taking great delight in his victories over Saul and the Philistines – and yes, the language and images are rather too graphic and violent for modern Christian sensibilities. I suppose that this is an example of 'youthful exuberance' from the new king, and perhaps we can forgive him a little of his over-excitement...

>After all, it is very important to remember what David used to be – a shepherd boy from Bethlehem. This part of the psalm shows an almost childlike wonder of what God has done – the whole experience of winning victories (v 37–42), ruling over many nations (v 43) and even having people obey him (v 44) must have been completely mind-blowing.

>It would have been so easy to have taken the glory for everything like so many of the Old Testament kings! But David was quick to give the glory to God (v 46–50), which is something we can definitely learn from. It's all too easy to lurch from crisis to crisis – David did enough times – but let's not forget to praise God for keeping us afloat!

>Think about the occasions that God has given you the victory in any situation. Write a song, poem or psalm and give him the glory – he deserves it!

I am not King David

I am not King David.

I have not watched my flocks at night,
Or slain a giant man,
I cannot play the lyre or harp,
Or sing as David sang.
I don't think I will be the king,
Or hunted by his army,
I will not have a traitor-son,
Or wives that drive me barmy.

Yet I too have been close to God,
But not opened my eyes;
I've shouted 'help!', I've shouted 'praise!',
And lots and lots of 'whys?'
I've shouted, screamed, poured out my heart,
And given grudging trust,
And I've met David's enemies,
Of pride, and pain and lust.

No, I am not King David, Lord,
And his songs to you aren't mine,
And yet I think you wish that
I would sing his songs sometimes.
For across the hundreds and thousands of years,
There stretches common ground,
And in these ancient psalms of praise,
My songs of love are found.

© James Lovelock

Single = miserable?

Decompress

'Holy God, I don't know what you have in store for me, but I want to serve you. Give me the help I need to continue, and bring people around me that will help me to know you better.'

Now read Corinthians 7:25–40

Immerse

I came home late last night and noticed two slugs on my doorstep who had decided that it was mating season. It's like they were saying to me, 'You loser, you are single – no one wants to mate with you. You are alone.' And it's true. I haven't married. Nor have I chosen to be single. (It just worked out that way.)

>The media constantly tells us we aren't complete unless we are either with someone or having sex with lots of people. We live in a society of wrecked marriages, bruised emotions and broken relationships. Many suffer terribly from the pain of past mistakes. If you are looking for a neat, clean, easy, black and white 'Christian' answer, to this, then there isn't one. But Paul gives us some recommendations.

Re-engage

Being single is actually a blessing in many ways. It gives you the opportunity to discover yourself. This is no mere thing! The surprising thing is, you are likely to find that you're not alone. Make the effort to get to know your friends, family, acquaintances, people in your church and be prepared to learn about yourself. When I am not being morose and feeling sorry for myself, I've discovered how amazing my friends can be, despite what I am like. I have been surprised by my family (and you know what family can be like) and how supportive they can be. I have learned much about how to be a human being from those around me in church.

>Don't be obsessed with the culture around you that demands we must have a partner. Let God provide in his time when you are ready. In the meantime you have the opportunity to grow in him and serve him. When it is time, God will let you know. Speak to him!

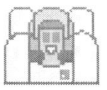

A meaty problem

Decompress
'Lord, have mercy on me, because I think I know better than others…'

Now read 1 Corinthians 8:1-13

Immerse
These days if you want meat, you go down to the butchers. It's been professionally slaughtered with minimal pain to the animal (so they tell me), prepared in a manner safe for human consumption and kept refrigerated so it keeps from rotting.

>In ancient times, not having the benefits of our refrigeration system, the only way to get fresh meat was to go someplace where it was killed and consumed on a regular basis. That would be your local pagan temple. Since you were in the temple anyway, you could also go and visit a temple prostitute to expunge yourself of your mortal sins. (At least that was the theory they had.) And you thought Tescos was convenient?

Re-engage
Often, as Christians, we can get pretty self-righteous about what we are allowed to get away with. I used to mock a friend of mine who refused 'as a Christian' to see certain movies (with perhaps a bit of nudity, bad language or violence – nothing overly serious) until I realised that he had a problem with pornography. I used to tease a friend of mine about her abstinence from alcohol, until she rebuked me once and told me she was a recovering alcoholic. I don't drink in front her anymore. I frequently taunt other friends whom I know are trying to keep to a diet by waving chocolate at them. I am probably going to get told off for that too one day.

>Luckily, I never caused any of these people any real damage (just irritation). But what if I really caused someone to stumble because of my stubborn insistence that I am allowed to do this because it is not forbidden by my faith? Maybe I already have and don't realise it.

>Think about the things you buy, eat, drink, smoke, watch and say. What are you representing to those around you? Don't be false, but ask yourself if your words, actions or the general way you live your life is actually helpful to those around you.

>It's simple really. Be mindful of those around you, and put them before you. (I always fail at this, so if you are like me, you should probably be asking God for forgiveness and asking him for the strength to start again about now.)

Airlock: Continuing

Giving due respect

C/23

Decompress

'Lord, help me to think about our church leaders with your thoughts. Help me to be less cynical and more positive in any criticism I may have.'

Now read 1 Corinthians 9:1-14

Immerse

Chances are that some of you are not always overly impressed by the leadership in your church. In the past I have been used, cut down, humiliated and treated dismissively by certain people who were supposed to be ministers of the Gospel.

>Paul deals with some serious issues here. People are questioning his authority by saying that he isn't really an apostle because he is not 'one of the twelve.' He tells the church in Corinth that they are the evidence of his apostleship. Therefore, because he is an apostle, he has a right to be treated in a certain way by other believers.

>Your church leaders are not perfect, but they are the leaders in the church and deserve a certain amount of respect. At the end of the day, they are the leaders and the people that God has entrusted, through the anointing of the Holy Spirit, with the shepherding of your local fellowship. Regardless of what we think of them, they are in charge. And they are important – we need them. You and the people in your church are evidence of their work. Most church leaders I have met are overwhelmed by the awesome responsibility this entails.

Re-engage

Leaders in the church are entrusted with an awesome task – namely the spiritual well-being of their congregation. They especially need your prayers. They need your help. Paul talks about the rights of an apostle – and among the things he lists are material things. How should they live?

>Ideally they shouldn't have to work, but be able to have their families be supported by their congregations. This is not always easy, especially if the congregation is small. Many of you may be thinking that you cannot make significant financial contributions (but reconsider whether you really do need all the things that you want to buy). There are other ways you can help – with your time for example. Decide how you will help.

Airlock: Continuing

The rights stuff

C/24

Decompress

Want to be a leader? Do you feel 'called'? Are you sure?

Now read 1 Corinthians 9:15–27

Immerse

Previously, Paul has stated quite flatly that as an apostle he is entitled to a nice two garage suburban house, a company car and a good salary (OK, those aren't his exact words, but you get the idea.) Now he tells us that he refuses all these things because he doesn't want his ministry to be an obligation (ie work for the reward he gets) but because he wants the (spiritual) reward from the work he wants to do.

>In this way, he is free from obligation. And because he has no obligations, he is free to go where he wants, to preach to who he wants, and become all things to all people, adapting to them and their situation.

>Paul's ministry is one of self-sacrifice and humility. Even though he was a free Roman citizen, able to travel where he wanted, he would make himself the equivalent of a slave – the lowest of the low – if it was beneficial to bringing people to the Lord. This isn't just about giving up material wealth, but about position and reputation in society.

Re-engage

Paul's ministry required great humility and flexibility and discipline. What are you willing to give up for Christ? To what extent are you prepared to serve others. We all have rights. But is it always beneficial to invoke them? Are you prepared to be wronged? Or to refrain from having to defend or justify yourself when you are wrong? Are you willing to accept that you are likely to be treated less than your worth for the sake of the gospel? Are you willing to risk your reputation?

>Can you relate to people from the whole spectrum of society? Or do you find certain people intolerable? Can you empathise with their situation? Can you put aside political, theological, ethnic, cultural or whatever differences in order to serve God? Would you be willing to work tirelessly without a lot of thanks for the trouble?

>If you think you can, have you considered entering into Christian ministry? Consider the tremendous sacrifices that people in ministry make. This makes me think twice about criticising them, but also makes me think that I need to re-evaluate my opinion even of those leaders that I don't like. Pray for your leaders now. In fact, pray for them every day.

Airlock: Continuing

Resisting temptation

Decompress

'Lead us not into temptation but deliver us from the evil one.'

Now read 1 Corinthians 10:1-13

Immerse

Many Christians I know tell me they wrestle greatly with temptation. It isn't wrong to be tempted, it's human. The temptations that we face are not evidence of poor moral fibre, or that you are a worse Christian than the one next to you at church – it is evidence that you have a pulse. You're alive!

>Of course, not all Christians are as severely tempted as others. Or at least, not all Christians are tempted in the same way. We all experience our Christian life uniquely. In this passage, Paul is referring to the rather lax attitude to sexual relations and idolatry, which in Corinth were very closely linked.

Re-engage

Why is it that I almost always fail miserably as a Christian when faced with ordinary life? After all, God has given us the strength to follow his will. In times of temptation he always gives us an escape route. Pray that he will give you the wisdom to find it in times of temptation.

>The very issues that the Corinthians dealt with are the same ones that we deal with today. We are being encouraged in our society, media and pop culture to 'live like Corinthians'. Our God, however calls us to holiness and purity. Grace will not protect us from making our own mistakes, but grace will help us to recover from them.

>Paul begins the passage using an allegory. He shows the example of Israel as baptism and communion. We are baptised into Christ's death, burial and resurrection. We partake of his body and blood in Communion – for the remission of sins. We are to put off the old self which has died. Now we are capable of living the life of Christ. We are partakers of his divine nature. This is God's grace.

>As members of this new life, we have God's promise that he will not let us endure more than we can handle. He has given us a way out. We need to ask for wisdom to find it. But if you fail, remember…

>God is continually calling us back to him. He is merciful and loving and committed to bringing about a transformation in you that you can only begin to imagine. Praise him because his mercy endures forever!

The temptation the Corinthians faced was living in their own city. It was famous for its temple prostitutes, drunken carousing, and fiendishly corrupt morals. Imagine Las Vegas, Reno, Blackpool and Bangkok all rolled into one. The place was so renowned for its debauched lifestyle that people all over Asia Minor would use the term 'to live like a Corinthian' or to 'Corinthianise' as a term to mean giving one's lecherous libido licence to live lasciviously. Becoming a Christian in this city virtually meant giving up being a Corinthian.

Sometimes it can feel like we're living in Corinth – suggestive adverts on billboards, explicit programmes on television, lewd lyrics on the radio, the different attitudes and expectations of our peer group...

How do you live a holy life in the 21st Century?

Extra_1 Jeremiah 26:1–24
Extra_2 Ephesians 5:1–20

Cheating

C/26

Decompress

'Lord God, help me to stay close to you, not just now in prayer and looking at your Word... but in everything.'

Now read Hosea 9:1-9

Immerse

I was 19, it was a dismal day and I'd finally managed to track down my girlfriend and drag her back to my room on campus to talk. She'd been avoiding me for a few days, and I knew something was wrong. It turned out she'd been seeing another guy behind my back for over a week. I was devastated – I couldn't believe that I'd been betrayed so badly. I spent the next few weeks wandering around feeling miserable, stupid, and angry.

>In this passage, God's feeling much the same way about the people of Israel. They're cheating on him – in fact, God says that they're selling themselves like prostitutes – with other, false, gods.

>Cheating on God is like cheating on the one you love. It becomes easier the more you do it, and you don't want to hear about it when someone catches you and tries to tell you that what you're doing is wrong.

Re-engage

We've got to remember that it really hurts God when we turn away from him and find other things to worship. In many ways, it's less simple today than it was in Hosea's day, because there's so many other things we can end up worshipping – money, the things we own, our relationships – all kinds of stuff can keep us from God. We've got to be aware that when people say that they've got no God at all, they may actually have other things to worship.

>This can be a problem with Christians, who are just as much God's people as the people of Israel were in Hosea's day. We often fall prey to worshipping other things above God, and the more we do it, the less we notice that we're doing it.

>Ask yourself: is your relationship with God everything that it could be? If it isn't, is there something coming between you? Although this is a specific action it may take more than just a quick, 'Yeah, X is coming between me and God, so therefore I'll get rid of/ stop doing/say goodbye to X.' Deepening your relationship with God may take time. So don't give up. After all, look how many prophets were used to try and bring Israel into line.

Airlock: Continuing

Sold out!

Decompress

'Father God, bring me close to you today, and help me to stay there.'

Now read Hosea 9:10–17

Immerse

We've all seen the movie where one of the good guys, for whatever reason, goes over to the other side and sells out the rest of the heroes. There's usually little hope of redemption for a character like that – in most cases, the traitor comes to a sticky end.

>In this passage, it's an entire country that's gone over to the Dark Side, and it looks like the result of betraying God and doing all kinds of evil things is going to be disaster.

>The difference between this story and the movies, of course, is that when the people of Israel realise what they've done wrong and come back to God, God will take them back – but first comes the bad news.

>People may have sold out God long ago, and might be doing just fine – it doesn't necessarily follow that if you're not following God, things will be bad for you – but in the end, there's only one result of turning away from God. And it isn't pretty.

Re-engage

In a sense, just by being fallible and broken humans, we've all betrayed God – but even as Christians, when we're sure that God has forgiven us for all the bad in our lives, we can find ourselves slipping away from God and playing with the dark side. Before we know it, we've stopped being pleasing to God (just like Israel in verse 10) and we're nowhere, with no idea how to get back, even if we want to.

>If you're reading this and your relationship with God isn't what it could be, it could be time to take a look at yourself and think hard about what you see. If you're going strong with God – that's great. But don't get complacent. Even the strongest of Christians can fall. Pray. Cultivate kindness. Strive to be like Jesus in everything. If you stick with it, you'll do just fine.

Idol thoughts

Decompress

'Lord God, help me to worship you and you alone.'

Now read Hosea 10:1–15

Immerse

It's a real problem with me – it always has been. I just get absorbed in stuff. And sometimes this stuff can be really stupid. TV shows, this book I'm reading and I just can't put down, my CD collection (although it's a really good collection, mind), PlayStation 2 (don't underestimate the power…), all the stuff I have to do in the house… all of this stuff can be the most important thing in my life at that particular moment.

>In the passage, God's upset by Israel's insistence on worshipping other gods, ones made of wood and stone. These days, there isn't much call for people to worship statues – but life can throw up so many other things which we can end up worshipping instead of God.

>The result of not worshipping God is that we start thinking that we can do things in our own power (let's face it, pop idols aren't going to be much help). The people of Israel made that mistake (v 13) and ended up biting off more than they

could chew. We can do that too. I know I have.

Re-engage

Some of the Israelites who worshipped a calf-shaped idol (v 5) thought they were actually worshipping God. We can do this kind of thing ourselves in church – we can get so wound up in the music, in the way that the minister talks at the front and just with doing stuff that we end up not actually engaging with God. Of all the ways in which Christians can go wrong, this is one of the easiest.

>There's nothing wrong with enjoying life. What's wrong is when something becomes more important than anything else, and more important than God. Think about the things you have and the things you do – could you manage without them? If you honestly don't think you could, you may have an idol there. It may be a case of saying, 'I will do without this for one day.' Get control of the things you do, then you can always make sure God is first.

Airlock: Continuing

Take you back

C/29

Decompress

'God, thank you that you'll always take me back, no matter what I do. Help me to give some of that love back to you and to the people around me.'

Now read Hosea 11:1–11

Immerse

In soap operas, people seem to fall in and out of love at a frightening rate, and even the best relationships can fall apart at any moment. People cheat, lie and change partners like they're playing musical chairs. And when relationships do end, there doesn't seem to be any chance of things getting back together again. Even when there's an exception, it usually goes horribly wrong.

> It's a relief to know that our relationship with God doesn't have to be like that. When we stray from him, we can always come back; if we genuinely want to be reconciled, he will always take us. He never stops loving us, and never gives up on us, even though we might stray again and again.

> The passage demonstrates this – although the people of Israel have done some terrible things, and have yet to go through all kinds of suffering, God is not going to abandon them. The difficulties they face are soon going to come to an end, and God's love for Israel remains constant, even though the people are not faithful to him.

Re-engage

If you've been reading through the book of Hosea with *Airlock*, you'll be aware of just how awful Israel was when the book of Hosea was written, and just how wonderful God's love was to put up with Israel, and even to promise to rescue the people when things went wrong. This is the same love which would eventually lead to God giving Jesus to the world, and the same love that would lead to Jesus' death on the cross. The same love which is offered to us… now… today.

> Spend some time thanking God for his love to you, and think about ways in which you can demonstrate and reflect God's love to the people around you. Been badly done by? Betrayed? Cheated on? It's hard, but try to forgive the people who have done this to you. Move on.

Airlock: Continuing

You'll never walk alone

C/30

Decompress

'Lord, help me to understand your words and then give me the strength to act on them.'

Now read Hosea 11:11 – 12:14

Immerse

I've got a friend who supports Swansea City Football Club. I can't help thinking that's a little misguided, maybe, but you can't fault her dedication. She's been behind the Swans ever since she was little, and has a season ticket. For as long as I've known her, she's never missed a home game. Now Swansea City are appalling. They never, and I mean never, win anything of note, and relegation isn't so much a fear as a grim certainty, but they're her team, and though they'll let her down, she's never abandoned them and never will. In a world where the team that wins the most stuff and has the most glamorous players gets all the supporters, you've got to give that sort of dedication the respect it's due.

>God's relationship with Israel in this passage seems to work on similar grounds. God's people in Israel haven't exactly been winners – Israel has let God down repeatedly – and in a much more profound way than a football team, what with the worshipping of other gods, the injustice and the dishonesty. But despite it all, God's still supporting them and is ready to bail them out when things go wrong.

Re-engage

God is faithful to us; history tells us so. Even if, like the people of Israel, we wander away, he remains faithful to us. But we've still got to respond to what God's saying, if we're really going to get the best out of the relationship If we don't, we're just like Israel in the passage, 'chasing the wind'.

>God hasn't let you down, but have you at any point let down God or the people around you? If you have, think about how you can put things right. Pray about it. And do what you can to sort things out. Say you're sorry. Make a phone call. Send an email. You get the idea. A few words can make the world of difference.

Airlock: Continuing

If you've done something wrong to someone, and you apologise, how can you be sure that you're going to be forgiven?

Does it make a difference if God's the one doing the forgiving?

Extra_1 Ezra 9:1–9
Extra_2 Isaiah 1:18–20

Faith laundry

Decompress

When someone says 'Let's pray', what do you do? Close your eyes? Bow your head? Run your fingers through your hair as if you were about to shampoo it? (Have you ever asked yourself why you do that?)

Now read Matthew 9:14–17

Background

Wineskins were just what they sound like - bags of animal skin that were used for storing and dispensing wine. New wine was always put into brand new wineskins because it would continue to ferment while it was inside the skin. A new skin was able to stretch around the wine. If new wine was put in an old wineskin, the old skin wouldn't be able to stretch anymore and would burst, ruining the wine and the skin.

Immerse

The disciples were having a fantastic time – living with Jesus, hearing his teaching first-hand, seeing miracles and healings take place. No wonder they weren't fasting. When asked why not, Jesus talked about wineskins to show that the legalism of the Old Testament wasn't necessary any more. It wasn't that he was against fasting, just that he thought people should choose to do it because it had real meaning for them, not because they had got into the habit of it.

>Jesus' teaching was all about grace – not having to earn your way into the kingdom of heaven, but knowing that you are there because you are loved by God. Once you have experienced the amazing love of God, you'll want to worship him, and that may well include fasting. But God's grace comes first.

Re-engage

Think about the way you worship God or pray and ask yourself why you do it like that? Are you hanging on to old habits that have lost their meaning? Indulge in a little 'faith laundry' and throw out any old unhelpful ways of doing things. Try something new in its place – go for a walk when you pray instead of sitting still; write out your prayers instead of saying them in your head; meet with a friend to pray instead of praying on your own.

What do you want?

Decompress

WWJD 4 U or
What do you want Jesus to do for you?

Now read Matthew 9:18–26

Immerse

When my nephew was 3, he really got into the idea of birthdays, especially receiving presents. Every time anyone came to the house, his opening comment was not 'Hello' or 'Welcome' or even 'How are you?' but 'Have you got a present for me?' It was totally embarrassing for his parents, but it showed his high levels of expectation. Why shouldn't everyone want to give him a present?!

Re-engage

In Jewish law, women were considered 'unclean' during their monthly period (Leviticus 15:19-24). This may seem very unfair to us – after all periods are a natural, normal thing. But the laws emphasised God's holiness and how hard it was for the Israelites to live up to God's standards on their own. The woman who touched Jesus had been bleeding for 12 years, and had been permanently unclean during that time. She would have been a social outcast because anyone she touched would also have become unclean. Imagine what an incredible difference touching Jesus made to her life.

>Both the synagogue leader and the woman who was bleeding had high expectations of Jesus. They were both faced with horrible circumstances. They didn't stop to think 'Am I worthy?', 'Have I been good enough?' or 'Will Jesus bother with me?' They just knew that Jesus was the answer to their problems. They weren't overwhelmed by the enormity of their circumstances; they just had high expectations of Jesus, based on what they had seen him do.

>Look back through these first few chapters of Matthew and make a list of all the things that Jesus has done that might raise your expectations of what he can do for you. Sit down with the list and praise Jesus for these things.

>Reminding ourselves of Jesus' power and compassion can raise our expectations of how he might intervene in our lives, but the opposite is also true. If you have felt let down, or feel like God hasn't answered your prayers, you may find it difficult to ask for things in prayer. If this is your experience, find someone to talk it through with, and ask them to pray for you.

Can you keep a secret?

C/33

Decompress

Imagine. A letter arrives through the post telling you that you've won a widescreen TV and a DVD player in a competition. What's the first thing you would do?

Now read Matthew 9:27–31

Immerse

The blind men called Jesus 'Son of David', which showed they believed he was the promised Messiah who would be descended from the great King David. Using this name for him showed great faith on their part.

>So why did Jesus tell these two men to keep quiet about their healing? You'd have thought that he would have wanted to everyone to know about the miracles he was performing. We aren't told and can only guess. But maybe Jesus didn't want people to get the wrong idea about his mission. He wasn't there to entertain crowds or do magic tricks; he was there to bring about the kingdom of God.

>He already had crowds of people following him around, and although he loved to heal he also wanted to teach his disciples and preach the good news about the kingdom without being swamped by people all the time.

>You can understand why the ex-blind men wanted to tell everyone the amazing news that they had been healed and could see. But Jesus also wanted people to understand that he could give them, and everyone, eternal life too.

Re-engage

Who would you have told first if you had won that competition? Your parents? Your best friend? Everyone you know? Why not send them a text message or an email and tell them some good news about Jesus instead?

>If we're honest, most of us have the opposite reaction to the blind men when it comes to telling other people about what Jesus has done for us – instead of wanting to make a big noise, we keep very quiet. What is it that stops you telling people about Jesus? What can you do about it? Pray about it, asking God to give you the confidence to tell people about him.

Airlock: Continuing

I've got the power

Decompress

Who or what do you have power over? How do you use that power?

Now read Matthew 9:32–34

Immerse

The Pharisees asked themselves a good question, but they came up with completely the wrong answer. They wanted to know where Jesus got his power. They concluded that because he had authority over demons, then he must have been given power by the prince of demons. But how does that make sense? Isn't that like Alex Ferguson telling Manchester United to go out and lose a match? If Jesus had been on the side of evil, he wouldn't have spent his time casting out demons, would he? The Pharisees just didn't want to admit that Jesus' power could come from God.

>The New Testament has lots of cases of Jesus casting out demons, but it's not something that we come across very often today. Why do you think that is? It could be partly that we are not as aware of spiritual matters and too quick to explain things as physical or mental illness. But it could also be that the prime purpose of Jesus' earthly ministry was to overcome the power of Satan, and to redeem people and God's creation from the effects of sin. And so there was more obvious and open conflict between Jesus and evil spirits while Jesus was on earth.

Re-engage

It's significant that when Jesus cast out the demon, the man got his voice back. You have the power to change situations even though you may not feel very powerful, just by joining your voice with others and making your opinions heard.

>Log on to www.tearfund.org/ youth for example, to see how you can get involved to help the world's poor.

>Log on to www.csw.org.uk to find out how you can get involved to help Christians who are being persecuted overseas.

>Are you 18 or over? Are you registered to vote in local and national elections? If the answers are 'yes' and 'no', then you should consider making the most of your voice by registering and voting.

>Do you use your voice to pray for God to heal people? Do we expect more from doctors than we expect from God?

Airlock: Continuing

Mission possible

C/35

Decompress

'The belief that God will do everything for man is as untenable as the belief that man can do everything for himself. It too, is based on a lack of faith. We must learn that to expect God to do everything while we do nothing is not faith but superstition.'
Martin Luther King

Now read Matthew 9:35–38

Immerse

This headline was spotted in a neighbourhood newsletter:
'Crime and Disorder – we all have a part to play'

>You kind of know what they meant to say, but this may have the opposite meaning to the one they intended!

>Jesus saw that the crowds were hurting and helpless, like sheep without a shepherd, but he knew he was the answer to that. He called himself the good shepherd in John 10:11 and said that he would lay down his life for the sheep.

Re-engage

It's interesting that Jesus' response to the crowds was not 'Wow, I've got so much to do here, I must work harder.' It was to pray that more people would join him in doing the 'harvesting', in bringing people into the kingdom. There's a paradox here – Jesus is the only one who can bring salvation to all these people. He is God's son and prepared to die for these 'sheep'.

>No one else can do that. But at the same time he can't do it on his own. Just before he died he told his disciples, 'anyone who has faith in me will do what I have been doing. He will do even greater things than these because I am going to the Father.' (John 14:12)

>Jesus needs his disciples to be involved; he needs you and me to be involved. Write down the names of people in your family, school, work or community who don't know Jesus. Pray and ask God to send people to introduce them to Jesus. Be prepared, though, to be the answer to your own prayer!

>How have you already been involved in bringing in the kingdom of God?

Airlock: Continuing

'With great power comes great responsibility.'
Peter Parker,
Spider-Man

These readings from Matthew 9 are a great excuse to watch *Spider-Man* again. Get some friends together and look out for the above quote.

How responsible are you?

Extra_1 Judges 16:23–31
Extra_2 Luke 4:14–30

Well well well!

Decompress

When was the last time you had a falling out with a friend? What was it about? How did you feel? Did you sort things out? Are you still friends?

Now read Genesis 21:22-34

Immerse

King Abimelech's servants have pinched a well which Abraham dug - possibly because they are picking on the weaker next door neighbour. Abimelech is the big man and has got more clout than Abraham, but that doesn't stop our hero from talking about his grievance - he's polite but firm about the business with the well. And Abimelech - who knows nothing about what his naughty servants have done - is mortified and sorts things out.

>Although Abimelech is the more powerful chap and is the big cheese, he's impressed by what he's seen of how God has looked after Abraham. Size isn't everything! And it's Abimelech who makes the first move for the treaty.

>Abraham is learning to trust God - his promise of land and kids seems to be coming together. He's still a traveller of no fixed abode, but he is learning that God is his protector - that God is stable and permanent, even if things are changing around him. As we walk with God, we learn to trust him too. God isn't tied to a particular place (a town, a country, or a building) and God will stick with us as the stable and permanent fixture in our lives, despite what else is going on round us - like moving schools, or houses, or parents splitting up or even Scunthorpe still not winning the FA cup...

Re-engage

If you and your friends (or your parents) fall out over something, here's two options you could try: 1) Pretend it never happened, let the thing fester and end up hating your mates and becoming all bitter and twisted inside. Or 2) Try and talk things through and reach an understanding. Can they see things from your viewpoint? Can you see things from theirs? Guess which way is best? Guess which option Abraham would choose?

>Have a think about the people who have power in your life. Are you frightened of them? Do they ignore you? Why not pray for them, once a day for the next few days and see what happens.

Airlock: Continuing

Lamb chops save the day

Decompress

Before you start to read today's note, be prepared that God may talk to you. He could ask you to do anything – and I mean anything!

Now read Genesis 22:1-19

Immerse

Families are not always the easiest of things – Abraham has already been tested to see whether he loved God more than his father (Genesis 12:1); now he's tested to see if he if he loves God more than his son. This is the tenth (and most difficult) trial Abraham has to face. But why would God – who had forbidden murder, hated child sacrifice and had promised descendants through Isaac – test Abraham like this, with no apparent explanation or reason?

>Maybe we should see the whole thing as part of a bigger picture. The nation of Israel was founded on these episodes of faithfulness, and the pattern was straightforward – God kept his promises, human beings trusted perfectly in them and were blessed.

Re-engage

God asked Abraham to do the unthinkable – his word is absolute, his reasons not given and his final word is grace. Sometimes we may feel that we are faced with impossible things: being a Christian at school or college, an exam or a big sports match, having to stand up in front of others etc. Whatever we face, we're unlikely to have to do anything like execute a member of our family. We should still approach things as Abraham did, trusting in God, who keeps promises.

>Isaac asked a good question: 'Where's the lamb for the sacrifice?' When we come to worship, what is the 'sacrifice' we offer? A sacrifice, by definition, is something which is costly and dear, not cheap and valueless. What are we sacrificing to God day by day? Iona's Wild Goose worship group liturgy uses the statement: 'I will not offer to the Lord sacrifices which cost me nothing.'

>What sort of sacrifices do you make for God?

Airlock: Continuing

Tomb with a view

Decompress

What's been the most crushing experience of your life? Have you ever felt as though life has completely knocked the stuffing out of you?

Now read Genesis 23:1-20

Immerse

It's a touching story of how Abraham grieves for his wife. They were knocking on in years (she was 127) yet they clearly loved each other deeply. He's old, he's a foreigner, he's growing in importance, he wants to trade with the natives, and yet he's not afraid to weep and wail in front of them. Notice that in Genesis, it's only the strong men who weep. (Look at the story of Joseph – on one occasion he wept so loudly that people outside his palace heard him! (Genesis 45.2)). Real men don't cry? What's the shortest verse in the Bible? John 11.35. What does it say? Still think real men don't cry?

>Although Abraham has been blessed and protected by God, although he's had many spiritual and physical highs, although he's shown tremendous faith and trust in God, although he's faced up to trials and come sailing through them, even Abraham is not immune to the pain of being human. Grief and bereavement are part of being human and if you've never experienced them yet, you will. Faith doesn't prevent bad or disappointing things happening, but it does give us a framework of understanding and a glimpse into the character of God, whose only Son also died.

Re-engage

Everyone dies eventually. However much you love somebody, no one lives forever. It's one of the facts of life. Because of the resurrection faith which Jesus handed on to us, Christians have always seen death, not as the end, but as the gateway to new life, living in glory and being with God in the Promised Land. That doesn't stop us being very sad and crying (like Abraham), over the death of someone close to us, and it doesn't stop us missing the person who's died, but it does help eventually to put things in God's perspective.

>Do you know somebody who's recently lost a loved one? Spend some time today praying for people who've been bereaved, asking for God's comfort.

Airlock: Continuing

Blind date stormer

Decompress

Can you think of a time when you were in trouble and you asked for God's help to get through it? What happened?

Now read Genesis 24:1–26

Immerse

Finding the right girl or boy, the person who we want to be with for the rest of our lives, Mr or Miss Right, can cause us lots of pain and, in the long run, needless worry. Unfortunately our society, and especially the congregations in some churches, seem obsessed with making sure that each and every one of us has a partner.

>What we need to remember is that God is in the business of looking out for us. The first step in sorting out our relationship situation is to trust God and talk it through with him. (That includes everyone – straight, gay, eternally celibate, lustily chomping at the bit, everyone.)

Re-engage

The servant wasn't just making a bargain with God, there was a practical reason for asking that the potential bride wasn't self absorbed, vain and unhelpful. The servant wasn't just looking for a beautiful wife for Isaac, he was looking for someone with compassion, a practical woman, courteous, charitable to strangers and willing to roll up her sleeves and muck in. Romantic love was not his first concern, although he couldn't help but notice that she was one foxy chick (v 21)! In other words, looks aren't everything – some of us have got them, others (like me) haven't – but remember beauty is only skin deep. Personality, attitude and love for others is much, much, much more important. Maybe if we spent more time worrying about these attributes and less time worrying about our zits, greasy hair and big bum, the world would be a very different place!

>The servant thanked God for his success (vs 26,27). He didn't try and pass it off as a fluke, or as a result of his clever manoeuvring, or of being in the right place at the right time – he knew where his success came from. Archbishop Michael Ramsay once said 'Coincidences happen when I pray: they don't when I don't.' When the chips are down, we often ask for God's help, but when things work out, are we inclined to forget God, or to forget to say thank you?

Airlock: Continuing

Love at first sight

C/40

Decompress

Have a think about the last time you got excited about God. How often do you get excited about him as opposed to getting excited about a CD, say, or an upcoming party?

Now read Genesis 24:28–67

Immerse

You really get the idea that Abraham's servant was excited as he told his story about how God had answered his prayer, led him to this place and presented the gorgeous Rebekah as a bride for Isaac.

>What about your story of faith? How has God guided you to be where you are? You may have a story in which you can look back to a date or a place where you started to follow Jesus; or you may look back to a period of time during which you responded to God's love and Jesus grew in importance.

>Either way, your story hasn't ended yet – so are you still excited about what God's doing with you? What are you learning? Is it obvious where God is leading you? It took ages for me to find out what God wanted me to do and that has evolved over time! But – as

Abraham's servant discovered – telling your story does help you see where God has been working, and what the future might hold...

Re-engage

Get a piece of paper and a pen and write down your story of faith – or just jot down the highlights. You could even draw a graph. Think about the following:

>Who were the significant people who helped to make Jesus real to you?

>Were there specific times and events which were important?

>What have you learnt about God recently?

>Can you see where God might be calling you in terms of job/career etc?

>Can you see what sort of person God is moulding you into?

>When you've written it all down, try sharing it with an older Christian friend and see what they make of it.

Airlock: Continuing

God provides. Abraham was confident that God would sort out the subject for his sacrifice, and he did. Nobody who has trusted in God has found God to shortchange them on his promises. Often we forget that God provides so much for us. Try thinking about all the ways God has provided for you. Continue this list of things to be thankful for...

1 Shelter
2 Clothes
3 Warmth
4 Food
5 Friends
6
7
8
9
10
11
12
13
14
15
16
17
18
19
20

Extra_1 Psalm 116
Extra_2 1 Thessalonians 5:12–18

Run away!

C/41

Decompress

'Lord God, you seem to be more concerned about my safety than I am. I try to look after myself but more often than not, I don't realise where the real dangers lie.'

Now read 1 Corinthians 10:14–22

Immerse

What is it about us human beings that means we like to take risks? What is it about us that makes us so unbothered about danger? Often we're more interested in seeing how near to danger we can get without getting hurt. Or we seem completely unaware of the danger. We walk as near to the cliff edge as possible.

>The people Paul is writing to are doing the same. They are completely unaware of the dangerous situation they are in. They pretend to know what they're doing when they're going to feasts dedicated to idols, but they don't know the reality of what is going on. Paul's advice is characteristically to the point. 'Run away from the worship of idols.' It's so serious that it's more than something they *shouldn't* do as Christians who celebrate the table of the Lord (Communion), Paul actually says it is impossible to do both. They can't share in the Lord's table and the table of demons. It is like trying to run towards two places in opposite directions at the same time. As he will go on to explain, it is the choice between doing what you believe you have the right to do, and doing what is best for others. The freedom that comes from being a Christian is not a licence to do what you want, it is a liberation to do what you ought.

Re-engage

There can be only response – flee. Run away. Don't carry on in the dangerous way of living while you decide what to do because to do so means you are not in any way living the way Christ calls us to. To live in ignorance of danger does not excuse us, nor does it prevent us from harm. To do so will damage us as well as those around us.

>It would be all too easy to draw up a long list of things we know we do where our heart attitude is to see how near to sin we can get and still get away with it. Instead, prayerfully ask God to show you a specific area where you are failing. It might be in your attitudes to money, sex, drink and drugs, what we watch, where we go, what websites we look at. Whatever it is, don't just stand on the edge of what God says not to do. Stand as far away as you can!

Airlock: Continuing

It's my life

Decompress

'Lord Jesus, help me to point others to your example, and to you, Lord, with all of my life. Amen.'

Now read 1 Corinthians 10:23 –11:1

Immerse

'It's my life, I've get every right to decide what I do with it.' It's an argument which people use to justify all sorts of things. And it's at the heart of what Paul has to deal with in Corinth. Christians understood their freedom in Christ as meaning that they could do whatever they want. Some even resisted any suggestions otherwise by insisting it was their right.

>And this is where it all falls down, because as Paul says, 'Not all things are good for us to do.' Again, in straightforward language Paul says, 'Do not look out only for yourselves. Look out for the good of others also.' Whether it's first century meat which has been sacrificed to idols, or a 21st century booze-up at a party – the principle remains the same. Why? Because as Christians we are to do all things to the glory of God above everything else. If, as a Christian, I claim that my life is to be glorifying to God, how can this be the case if I am looking only to my own rights, and not the needs or sensitivities of others?

Airlock: Continuing

Re-engage

Let's be honest, it's all too easy to say 'I have every right to do this, say that, be whatever.' Even in church. It's my right to worship the way that means the most to me, even if the old people don't like it. It's my right to talk through the sermon or walk out if it's boring. It's my right to wear the type of clothes I wear for church, even if it causes a problem for other people.

>It might 'be our right' but that doesn't make it right, especially if it makes others go wrong. Paul's writing to Christians here – so we need to listen to what he says. As soon as we become more important in our own eyes than others, we can be sure our eyes are no longer on Jesus.

>Here's something radical. Why not try consciously, for a week, to ask yourself the question, 'Is this unhelpful, hurtful or harmful to others?', before you do anything that you'd normally do as a Christian? Doesn't matter if it's their problem or yours – just ask the question and let God speak to you. If you feel up to it, why not ask God at the same time what you could change in your life that would bring more glory to him?

A close shave

C/43

Decompress

'Lord, sometimes it's hard to make sense of bits of the Bible. Help me to understand not just what your Word says, but also why, so I can understand what it means for me and my friends today. Amen.'

Now read 1 Corinthians 11:2–16

Immerse

I recently heard of a group of Christian lads who showed their love for one of their youth group who had chemotherapy and had lost his hair by shaving their hair off and being bald with their friend. It meant the world to their friend, and I'm sure it touched God's heart too as they did something to practically show the love and glory of God to their friend, and to those around them.

>That's what is at the heart of this difficult part of Paul's letter. Practically showing the love and glory of God to others. Being willing to do something for no other reason than bringing glory to God. The issue is NOT God's preference in hairstyles or hats. It makes no difference whether men or women should have their heads covered or have long hair. Nor is it about women being subordinate to men or men being in authority over women. What it is ALL about is whether the way we live our lives points people to Christ or away from Christ. Our hairstyle ultimately doesn't matter – but our heart attitude towards others certainly does.

Re-engage

Let's be practical. If you drink, is your drinking causing those around you a problem? It might, it might not. But if you don't ask the question, you won't know the answer. And if the answer's yes, would you be prepared to stop drinking if it would help point people to Christ? You could ask the same about your attitude to relationships, money, possessions, what you watch on TV, DVD, video or the net. If anywhere in your heart the response is, "I've got every right to do this, that's their problem not mine", Paul's words are very much words you need to hear today.

>Pray. Think. Pray some more. Write down a list of things which, if God asked you not to do them, you'd have a problem because you'd want to do them. Why not see how many of the list you find yourself willing to give up?

Airlock: Continuing

How NOT to have a party

'Lord, help me to put you as the centre of all my worship; in all I am and all I do.'

Now read 1 Corinthians 11:17–22

Immerse

Parties – don't you just love them? But can you imagine a party where everyone is served the most amazingly delicious meal and you get a mouldy old piece of fish, a cream cracker, and some brown celery? They all have something nice to drink, and you have water from the toilet bowl. And to top it all, everyone talks to each other – and leaves you out. Not much of a party at all!

>Which seems to be pretty much what was happening in the church at Corinth. As if this wasn't bad enough, it was most evident during the church's celebration of Communion.

>Paul says that this attitude of the Corinthian Christians to eating meat sacrificed to idols is a total preoccupation with self at the expense of others. Paul points out that they may be going through the motions of taking Communion but they're missing the point – something he will shortly explain as having potentially fatal consequences!

Re-engage

Yeah I know, your church doesn't do anything like this. Neither does mine. BUT, I wonder how many divisions or grudges there are in the people in your church when they take Communion together. I wonder what things in your heart separate you from others? Communion is a really easy way to pretend to be in unity with people – what will you be thinking next time you take Communion?

>Why not get your youth group together, or some of your friends, and run a 'pot luck supper?'. The whole idea is to charge a set price, say £10, for a meal for a group of people. The menu for the meal is a range of different meals representing the food people in different countries may have for a main meal. The meals are chosen at random when the guests arrive. The contrast should be staggering – from a handful of rice through to a three course meal. Use your imagination for different meals. Why not get a missionary to come and join you and tell the group about a different part of the world. It's a great way of raising some money and brings home some of the inequalities we live with in our world.

Airlock: Continuing

The universal laws of glasses

C/45

Decompress

'Lord, let me see you more clearly as I read your words, and as I see you more clearly may I act in ways that are pleasing to your gaze.'

Now read 1Corinthians 11:23–34

Immerse

I've had glasses ever since I was three. Anyone who regularly wears glasses will be aware of the unwritten law of the universe that says if you ever get a splat mark on your glasses, it's always in the worst place and totally messes up your vision. Yet it's also an unwritten law of the universe that if you wear trendy sunglasses with a designer label etched into the lens, you never notice it. Why? Because in a short space of time, your eye adapts to the mark being there, and it cleverly adapts to this and ignores it. In other words, it appears to go away – yet in reality, it's still there.

>In the same way, our spiritual sight is subject to a similar universal law. Here Paul warns the Corinthians about the dangers of sharing in the meal commemorating Jesus if their heart is not right. This had led to sickness and in some cases even death!

>Back to our universal laws. If our spiritual sight is splatted with sin, our vision is messed up. It will affect our life, how we see ourselves, and what we do. At Communion we will be taking the body and blood of Christ in an unworthy way and in doing so will be sinning against Christ. We will also be bringing judgement on ourselves. Scary stuff, but not as scary as the second universal law. If we don't examine ourselves regularly, our spiritual sight gets used to the sin, and it's all too easy not to even know it's there.

Re-engage

Paul may be Mr Theology but he's also Mr Practical. Examine your own heart. Judge yourself. There's no escaping the fact that we have to take responsibility for ourselves, our own heart, and our own actions. 'Get real in other words', 'Don't go through the motions' says the Word of God. Jesus doesn't want lip service, or empty gestures. He wants heart service, and a life that flows from a heart that is daily being changed by the love of God.

>Find a piece of clear glass or even better, an old pair of glasses. Take a cloth and clean the glass or glasses and as you do, ask God's Holy Spirit to help you see your heart and yourself for what it really is. Ask him to help you see those things which your spiritual sight might have just got used to seeing.

Airlock: Continuing

Whenever we read any of the teaching in the Bible we face the dilemma – to what extent is this relevant for today or is it simply something just for 'Bible days'. And it's a crucial question. For example, In 1 Corinthians we have teaching on hairstyles and eating food sacrificed to idols, mixed in with teaching about sexuality, immorality, marriage, lawsuits and so on.

In this case it's an issue of rights. It appears that both Christian men and women in Corinth were more concerned at exercising their rights to do whatever they wanted – apparently to prove the point they could – than bringing glory to Christ. As already mentioned, Corinth embodied the principle 'Do whatever you want' so this insistence by Christians of having the right to do whatever they wanted was apparently causing problems for Christians and non Christians alike. Paul gives practical advice – for the Christians at Corinth to behave in a way that wouldn't point people away from Christ.

Are there instructions in the New Testament which you think genuinely don't apply to Christians today? If so, which ones, and why?

Extra_1 Colossians 3:16–23
Extra_2 2 Timothy 3:14–17

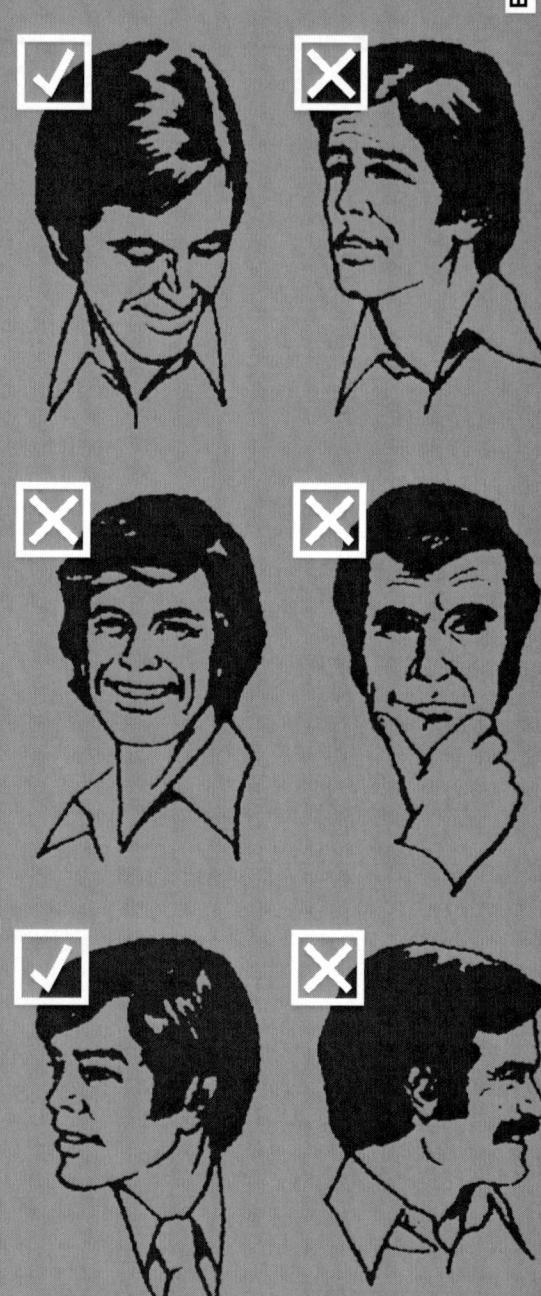

Animal lovers

Decompress

You said you wouldn't do it. In fact you promised you wouldn't do it. You didn't mean to do it. Then you did it. Dur. Think about an occasion when that was you.

Now read Hosea 13:1–16

Background

Although we talk of 'Israel' it was divided into two kingdoms in Hosea's time (eighth century BC). The northern one, sometimes confusingly called Israel, was named after one of the first tribes to settle there, Ephraim. Judah was the southern kingdom.

>Israel had originally demanded a king (like the other nations) despite God's assurance that they needed no king but the Lord. Verses 10 and 11 reprise God's anger at this.

>The foe that would conquer Ephraim was to be Assyria - a nation with a reputation for the sorts of brutishness listed in verses 15 and 16.

>Between 734 and 722 BC the northern kingdom of Israel and many of its neighbours were reduced to being insignificant, and unloved, parts of the mighty Assyrian Empire.

Immerse

Think of all the empires who have dominated the world at various times in human history from the ancient Egyptians to Coca-Cola. They're all unstable. The giants of one era can easily become the dwarfs of the next. But why? Usually the answer is human frailty. In our passage, the weakness was to shift the focus of worship from God to Baal. This is seen to be an unforgivable error.

>Imagine a world where every product advertised added the disclaimer that God was more important and was to be worshipped above all things or people.

Re-engage

Most of us are over-optimistic. Hosea has given his people cause for long-term hope but short-term disaster. Try and live your life over the next few days with a realistic assessment of how others will behave. If they do let you down, you will be ready.

>Complacency was Israel's downfall. Are there areas of your life in which you find it hard to avoid complacency? What could you do about that? Spend some time talking to God about those areas.

Airlock: Continuing

Second second chance

Decompress

As you get ready to read this passage, pray that you will be willing to make any changes to your life that it shows up. Never study the Bible without a willingness to live with the consequences.

Now read Hosea 14:1-8

Immerse

The film has set up the relationship. The meeting. The first kiss. Probably sex (there usually is). Then the misunderstanding. 'How could you?' The walk out. Tears. Loneliness. 'Come back!' The jilted lover shouts down the street to the departing partner. 'Come back! I love you. I never meant to hurt you.' Through Hosea, this is God's big shout out. Except he is the one who has been let down. He has been hurt.

>The only negative command in this whole passage is expressed in six words, '… have nothing to do with idols.' Everything positive in the passage that will happen in the future flows from obeying this simple rule, yet to date it has been a rule that has been beyond Israel's keeping.

Re-engage

Have you ever let God down? Put something else in his place? God wants nothing more than for you to come to your sense and return to him. Remember the Lost Son in Luke 15, who came to his senses in a pig-sty? It probably hasn't come to that yet, but God wants you back if you've wandered.

>Keep a record of everything you do for a day. At the end of the day reflect; was God in all of it? Were there times when you deliberately turned your back on him? What can you do to make sure that doesn't happen tomorrow?

>Verse 3 says 'We will not say again, "Our gods," to the things our hands have made.' Think about things you tend to place too much value in. Try imagining there's a fire in your house. You can grab one small possession. What would it be? Be honest now; do you over-value this thing. Thank God for it, whatever it is, and put him above it.

Airlock: Continuing

Get wise

Decompress

Wising up to God is a matter of life and death. Ever stopped to think that reading your Bible could save your life? Or that reading your Bible could save somebody else's life?

Now read Hosea 14:9

Immerse

We've reached the end of the book of Hosea. OK so what's happened? Hosea, bless him, has lived his prophetic life as a giant symbolic act. He's married a prostitute yet been required to remain faithful to her. He has given his children symbolic names. He's been required to speak out against the unfaithfulness of his people with the certainty of God's eventual judgement. He's given his all. The book ends with the promise of hope for the obedient. The Contemporary English Version of the Bible catches the force of the verse by pitching it in the form 'If you do A ... then B will happen'.

>If you are wise you will ... understand

>If you obey ... we will walk together, but

>If you are wicked you will stumble

>Bob Dylan once said, 'Nobody ever does what is right; they just do what they want and then repent.' There is some truth in that, but hopefully Christians should be trying to do what is right.

>This last verse of Hosea, a book which has seen the promise of dreadful judgement being acted out on God's people by a neighbouring, cruel army, asks them to change. Don't just do what you want then hope to repent; do what is right. Do it now.

>At his enthronement in February 2003, the new Archbishop of Canterbury, Dr Rowan Williams said. 'If someone approached you in the street and said, "They've found out; you'd better run," about 90% of the population would run.'

>What are you hiding? Of what do you need to repent?

Re-engage

It's repentance, repentance, repentance all the way today.

>Kneel in prayer.

>And/or

>If you share a truth with someone it won't be so scary if others find out too. Try repenting to a friend.

Airlock: Continuing

Nasty neighbours

C/49

Decompress

'Lord, help me understand your words. Make their meaning clear and help me act on what they teach me.'

Now read Obadiah 1–14

Immerse

Imagine twins who fall out. Whilst the dispute is about a very petty matter, over the weeks, months and years that follow they do not talk to each other. They both wait for the other sibling to make the first move. Eventually it takes a third party to get them to see sense. They won't talk to each other but they will talk to the outsider.

>Obadiah is a one chapter prophecy about the downfall of Edom, a kingdom to the south of Judah (which is to the south of Israel). Edom was a mountain kingdom approached through a narrow pass. This makes sense of verse 3. The people felt pretty safe there.

>Although there had been skirmishes between Israel/Judah and Edom over the years, Edom's crime seems to have been not helping and taunting more than actually being aggressive.

Re-engage

It's amazing how rivalries can escalate. Without demeaning the powerful words of God's prophet Obadiah in any way (his name itself means 'God-worshipper') it would be good to get ourselves a reputation for diminishing conflict rather than escalating it. Don't let things get out of hand.

>You do not always have to apologise for your behaviour to reconcile things, but you can be sorry that a situation has arisen. So don't say: 'I'm not apologising. It's all her fault.'

>Do say: 'Claire, I didn't mean this to lead us to fall out and I'm sorry this situation has happened. Can we talk about it please?' (Don't say Claire if the person is called Arthur, though. You'd look silly.)

>More difficult questions to think about: Why is it so much more fun to think about what you will do to make your enemies suffer than how you could stop them being your enemies?

>So what disputes are currently knocking around in your life? How could you resolve them?

Airlock: Continuing

Hammer time

Decompress

Imagine what it might be like to be on the receiving end of a prophecy about your destruction. Would it make a difference if you lived in one of the safest places on earth?

Now read Obadiah 15–21

Background

Remember Jacob and Esau? They were sons of Isaac. Their rivalry as brothers is told in Genesis 25-36. Israel was descended from Jacob; Edom from Esau. They never got on.

>In Psalm 137:7 the Edomites taunting when Jerusalem fell is mentioned. 'Tear it right down,' they said. Obadiah prophesies their comeuppance. The Edomites danced and drank as Jerusalem fell. When Edom is defeated, says Obadiah, people will drink (v 16) until Edom disappears altogether. It did.

Immerse

Complacency is probably the greatest enemy of the competent. Anyone preparing for an exam by thinking about how clever they are, rather than doing any revision, is probably heading for failure. Likewise going into a sporting contest being sure you are the better player can be a recipe for disaster – knockout games being won by underdogs, Wimbledon being won by unseeded players, independent candidates winning elections – all these things are the result of complacency by the strong. Pride, as the saying goes, comes before a fall.

>'You'll not get us…' say the Edomites, '…look where we live.' Word to the wise. NEVER tell God he can't get you. Risky strategy. VERY risky.

Re-engage

Search out complacency in your life and replace it with strategy. That may be a short sentence, but it could have huge consequences. So I'm going to repeat it! Search out complacency in your life and replace it with strategy.

>Try and do something this week that is beyond 'not interfering'. Get involved in righting a wrong. It may be something you need to look out for, or it may be something you know of already.

I intend to
move out to
the right
or turn right

'Road rage is caused by the
assumption that everyone else
will drive perfectly.'

Discuss.

Extra_1 Proverbs 1:7
Extra_2 Psalm 137

Mission not impossible

C/51

Decompress

God has a mission. And it involves you. Are you ready to find out your job?

>Sure?

Now read Matthew 10:1-15

Immerse

Driving a car for the first time is exciting but it can also be pretty scary.

>You've watched someone else do it for years. You've had someone sit there and explain to you how it's done. You've got it all sorted in your head. But now you have to put your own feet on the pedals, your own hands on the wheel, your own eyes on the road, and actually drive this thing yourself. (And ideally not run anyone over.)

>Jesus' followers have been watching and learning from him for ages. Finding out all about God's mission, and seeing it in action.

>Now in this passage, Jesus says, 'OK, enough of me – over to you. You watched, you learned. Now do.

>'You heard me preach my message, saw the way I lived. You went 'Ooh!' when I cast out demons, and 'Aah!' when I healed the sick. Now you have a go.'

Re-engage

Jesus sent his followers out to do the same things they had seen him doing: telling people the good news about God and making the world a better place.

>The same goes for us. We're on exactly the same mission. We may not have the power to do all the things he talks about here, but what can you do to fulfil his mission here and now? What kind of things did Jesus do that you can do too? What can you do to spread his message and make the world a better place? It may mean spending some time in prayer to work things through.

>There are many Christian organisations working to continue the work Jesus did. Why not visit one of these websites and find out how you can help?

>www.fish.co.uk
>www.oasistrust.org
>www.worldvision.org.uk
>www.scriptureunion.org.uk

Airlock: Continuing

Half-snake, half-dove

Decompress

Have you ever had to suffer because of your Christian beliefs? How would you cope if you had to choose between your life and your faith?

parts of the world persecution still goes on. In fact, in some parts of the world, it can be a life-threatening experience just to tell people that you're a Christian.

Now read Matthew 10:16–25

Immerse

I've never seen a dead body – unless you count woodlice. And frankly I'm happy to keep it that way. As far as I can see, a live body has everything a dead body has plus the fact that it moves around and does stuff, which it seems to me is the whole point of a body in the first place.

>I guess we're a bit soft these days where death is concerned. I don't suppose people died any more often in Jesus' day (just the once, I think) – but many people died younger, more unpredictably and often more violently.

>Jesus warns his followers that if they think they're used to dead bodies, they can think again. Being a Christian, he says is going to be a violent, hard and bloody experience.

>He was absolutely right. For the first few centuries Christians faced terrible attacks and thousands were killed. And in some

Re-engage

It's unlikely that you or I will ever have to face the kind of things that Jesus talks about here. But still it can be hard to take when we suffer – even in really small ways – for our faith.

>How willing are you to stand up for what you believe in when it costs you? Will you speak out when people don't like what you say? Why not thank God that you don't have to face serious persecution. Pray for those who do, and ask him to help you in whatever trouble you do face?

>Pay a visit to http://www.releaseinternational.org to find out more about Christians being attacked across the world and what you can do to help.

Stand and deliver

C/53

Decompress

'Lord, help me to look at the things, which take priority in my life.
Lord, give me the strength to give things the right priority in my life.'

Now read Matthew 10:26–42

Immerse

OK, this comment would work a lot better if I could remember what the film was called, or in fact anything much about it at all. But I'm over 30 and so my brain's dead. Anyway, there's a goody and a baddy, both trying to get to this treasure. When they reach it at the end, there's a massive flood and the goody swims for his life while the baddy sinks to his death because he won't let go of the treasure.

>See it if you get the chance – it's a great film.

>The point is that that's a pretty screwy bunch of priorities, dying rather than letting go of your treasure. And Jesus would certainly have said 'What a dum-dum.' And yet, he also says that your priorities should be just as screwy as that when it come to your faith. Nothing in your life should be as important as following Jesus. Not your possessions, or your family or even your life itself.

>He isn't saying that family shouldn't be important to you. The Bible says lots and lots about how we should respect and obey our parents, and take care of each other. So 99 times out of 100, following Jesus will mean doing what's right by your folks. When it comes to the crunch though, and you have to choose between doing what the family wants (or anything else) and staying true to Jesus, Jesus demands that we put him first.

Re-engage

Jesus' first followers knew for sure that he was their number one priority because they really did have to leave friends and family and face violent opposition because of him.

>It's harder for us to know because we're not faced with the same tough choices. So just how much do you think you would be willing to give up for him?

>Make a list of your favourites. Favourite possessions. Favourite people. Favourite activities. Say thank you to God for all these things you enjoy, and reflect on whether any are more important to you than Jesus. Ask him to help you put him first.

Airlock: Continuing

John's video shop disaster

C/54

Now read Matthew 11:1-15

Decompress

What kind of things make you doubt Jesus?

Now read Matthew 11:1-15

Immerse

'It's a fantastic film,' I tell them, as we stand in the video shop. 'One of the funniest films I ever saw. We should definitely get this film out. It's years and years since I saw it, but I totally loved it. Just trust me, OK, you'll be in hysterics.'

>So we watch it. And something terrible has happened since I first saw it. Either someone has taken every joke and replaced it with stupid no-brain rubbish, or I've grown up and hadn't noticed. I know that everybody in the room hates me and will probably make me eat the video. If only it was a DVD.

>Which is probably how John the Baptist feels, standing there in the desert in his trendy camel outfit, leg of BBQed locust caught in his beard. He pointed his thousands of fans to Jesus, and cried, 'He's the one! He's the Messiah we've all been waiting for! God's answer to all our prayers. Follow him!'

>The problem is that the Messiah was supposed to be a glorious leader who would make the nation great again. All Jesus seems to do is stand around in fields telling people about God and healing them. 'Errm, Jesus,' says John. 'Is it time for me to be very, very embarrassed yet?'

Re-engage

Do you ever feel like John? Ever feel that you expected Jesus to help you out, but he didn't? That you thought being a Christian would make more difference than it has? That he doesn't answer your prayers? That when you need him he's not there?

>What do you do about it? Maybe there's someone you can talk to. You could do a lot worse than what John did, which was to talk to Jesus and tell him about his doubts. When he did that, Jesus didn't tell him off and say he should have stronger faith. He pointed out all the good things that John had seen him do, and promised him he would be blessed by God if he didn't throw in the towel. Are there good things that Jesus has done in your life that you can look back to when things get tough?

>Why not talk to Jesus now? Tell him about the things you don't understand, and the things you think you do. Tell him about the things that make you doubt and the things that make you believe. Tell him about the things that upset you and the things that make you thankful.

Airlock: Continuing

Damned if you do...

Decompress

Have you ever felt that your relationship with God is different to other peoples? That you prefer different ways of worship, or have different ideas and opinions? No two Christians are quite the same. Take a moment to think about what makes you different.

Now read Matthew 11:16–30

Immerse

Jesus and John the Baptist both had beards, if I remember my Sunday school colouring lessons rightly, but then so did pretty much everyone else in the Bible, so that wasn't terribly controversial. What was controversial was their attitude to food. For John it was important to live the strictest possible life in order to be close to God. He took it so far that a lot of religious people said he was a complete maniac.

>Jesus, on the other hand, loved a good nosh up, washed down with a glass or two of homemade wine. 'Well, that's not very religious,' tutted people. Jesus could have explained why his way was right and everyone else was wrong. But he seriously respected John's way of living for God, so he didn't.

>So instead his answer was, 'John goes hungry, I party. So what? He has one way of living for God, I have another. We can't please you people, and we're not going to try, so you might as well stop judging us and let us go our own different ways.'

Re-engage

Think again about the way that you like to worship. To pray. Think about the way you believe you should live, and the things you believe about God. Are there people who try to persuade you to go their way? Do you try to persuade others to do it your way?

>It's essential to listen to other people, and learn from them. But in the end, the choice is yours – you have to go your own way, believe your own beliefs and live your own life.

>Write a spiritual profile of yourself. Who are you? What kind of Christian are you? What kind of church do you like? What do you like and dislike about you own church? What songs do you like? How do you pray? How do you worship? Do you live a strict religious life or relaxed? Who is God to you? Plus any more information you can think of.

Airlock: Continuing

> Don't go to the non-Jewish people or to any town where the Samaritans live.
> But go to the people of Israel, who are like lost sheep.
> When you go, preach this: 'The kingdom of heaven is near.'
> Heal the sick,
> raise the dead to life again,
> heal those who have skin diseases,
> and force demons out of people.
> I give you these powers freely, so help other people freely.
> Don't carry any money with you – gold or silver or copper.
> Don't carry a bag or extra clothes or sandals or a walking stick. Workers should be given what they need.

Do the instructions Jesus gives his twelve followers here apply to Christians today too? If he was sending out these followers today, do you think he would say the same thing?

Extra_1 Matthew 28:18–20
Extra_2 Acts 10:1–48

From heaven to earth

C/56

Decompress

Have a think about this quote from the famous mystic Thomas Merton: "By reading the scriptures I am so renewed that all nature seems renewed around me and with me. The sky seems to be a pure, a cooler blue, the trees a deeper green. The whole world is charged with the glory of God and I feel fire and music under my feet."

Now read Psalm 19

Immerse

This psalm is about how both nature and law point to God. A friend recently told me about a pagan he'd met. This guy had grown up in a regular church. One day he was out walking in some woods and as he encountered a sunlit clearing, he had a profound supernatural experience. He spoke to his Sunday School teacher about it, who said, "Don't ever do that again, that's nature worship." The guy claimed that if the teacher had reacted differently, he would probably be a Christian today instead of a pagan. Ouch...

Re-engage

For those of us who like an easy life, this psalm represents danger – new age mysticism on the one hand, and controlling Pharisee-style

Airlock: Continuing

religion on the other. Maybe that's why they've been put together... No, I don't think it's so they'll cancel each other out – quite the opposite. Jesus went out on to a mountain to pray, not into a room. Yet he also said we had to outdo the holiest people in their law keeping.

>Following Jesus is an extreme sport, but you can't go off in just one direction – you have to be extreme in everything, because that's the safest way to avoid being a fanatic. Love God through nature, sure, but love God through reading the Bible, too. It's not either/or, it's both/and. I love the way that the psalm uses the beauty of nature to describe the scariness of God, and talks about the law (pretty scary) as something beautiful... Don't allow yourself to become a fanatic – become an extreme Christian!

>If you are someone who tends towards studying the Bible then allow yourself to encounter God in the world too. Maybe take this psalm out into the countryside with you one day... If you're trying these notes because Bible-reading is hard for you, try doing it in places that make you feel good. If that's the countryside, why not give God a day and go for a walk with him, and take your Bible with you?

A prayer for a godly king

Decompress

How much do you pray for your government or for the people in charge? It's not something that we have a great deal of experience in nowadays (apart from that bit about praying for the Queen if you're an Anglican), yet it has been a central part of our faith going back to the days when this psalm was written.

Now read Psalm 20

Immerse

Today, although we still officially have a state religion, faith and politics are considered two different arenas which are best kept apart. Or at least that's what the politicians think, anyway. The last thing they want is Jesus interrupting their deals and double-crosses. We probably feel a tiny bit like the state of Israel feels today, and felt even in David's time: there are people out to get us, so how are we going to keep our children safe? This psalm is a big challenge to us: how can we trust an invisible God to save us from all-too-visible danger?

Re-engage

I think one important bit in this psalm is the gap in the middle – this is almost an entire worship service liturgy, except that we don't know what happens in the selah.. One possibility is that the selah section included readings about the great things that God had done in the past. Both of these seem great ideas to me: worship and forgiveness, as well as retelling the story of how good God has been to us.

>What we want is for our leaders to say with David, 'Now I know the Lord helps his appointed king. He answers him from his holy heaven and saves him with his strong right hand' (v 6). Pray for those who have power over you, that they will acknowledge Jesus as Lord, and that he wants to be Lord over their public life just as much as their private life. You might even want to write to a politician or civil servant that you know, and let them know the good things that God is doing in your community.

And after the battle... ?

C/58

Decompress

Where is God when countries go to war?

Now read Psalm 21

Immerse

This is a hymn revelling in Israel's past conquests and looking forward to its next victims. At best, I find it extremely uncomfortable to read such a psalm, and on first reading I wondered what we could learn from the kind of enjoyment of others' suffering that makes the present US administration look like St Francis of Assisi...

>Have you thought about what God is doing when people are at war? And – here's the one that I'm struggling with – is it possible that God doesn't like bits of this psalm too much either?

>This Psalm is big, it's brash, it's an uplifting of the king and then a focus on God who gives and demands all the glory. To me it feels a bit like a bunch of lads singing football chants on the terraces after their team has beaten a big rival. It has some relationship with Psalm 20, but we don't know exactly what. It might be another part of a special ritual for the king, like a coronation or a rededication, or it might be a ready-made celebration of victory in battle. The key is that the focus starts with the king and ends up very much on God. For all that we think the king is fantastic, he is what he is by the power and grace of God alone.

Re-engage

This psalm presents a God who gives a king everything he asks for, and yet also kills the children of his enemies. How does this image of God fit with what you know of him? This is no mere academic exercise. It impacts on how we should treat criminals, Iraqi prisoners of war (and their children), how we pray, what we pray for. When we read the life of David, we don't say to ourselves, 'David slept with another man's wife, so we should'. Maybe we need to have the same attitude to David's songs? David's priests sang songs about God killing the families of their enemies, but does it mean that we should?

Airlock: Continuing

From the heart of God

Decompress

This is one of those psalms you just want to leave all by itself. Lay out all your troubles before God and take your time reading this longer psalm. Let it soak into you and come out of you as prayer.

Now read Psalm 22

Immerse

This is the psalm that Jesus quoted on the cross. We don't know if he recited more than the first line, but we know that he knew where it was headed: through suffering and into praise. Jesus was referring to a psalm which ends, 'The people in the future will serve him; they will always be told about the Lord. They will tell that he does what is right. People who are not yet born will hear what God has done.' Wahey!

Check out how the mood changes from verse 23 onwards: the psalmist is expressing something new in the world of worship and theology, something that would only come to fruition when Jesus chose to be crucified. The idea here is that God is present in suffering and can make something amazing come out of it, that the person who suffers is special to God.

>Many, many Christians experience poverty and persecution. Yet they always seem to be the happy ones! This psalm presents a huge challenge to us as the wealthiest and most comfortable Christians who have ever lived. It is a testimony of golden praise that has been cast in the fires of hell. When we suffer from loneliness or depression, let's read this psalm together and recognise that our alienation is a comfortable equivalent of the pain the psalmist is going through.

Re-engage

God does not expect us to be happy all the time, and he wants us to express our feelings whatever they are. Do that now. Maybe you have feelings that you have never felt able to express to God before – anger, frustration, fear... you will find them all in the Psalms! Remember that this psalm finishes with this sentiment: 'I'm still here and I'm gonna praise you no matter what!'

Airlock: Continuing

A song of hope

C/60

Decompress

This one psalm has been a strength for millions and millions of people over the years. There are also far too many posters of little kittens with verses from this psalm in the world.

Now read Psalm 23

Immerse

Here's an idea: this song grew out of the writer's real life experience. Some of this poetry is about knowing that God is present even in the hard times, and it's those bits (particularly verses 4 and 5) which are about 'I' and 'you'. The first three verses speak about God as 'He'... I think this person's faith has come through a mega time of testing, but with a renewed understanding of who God is and what he's like.

>The contrast with the royal Psalms 20 and 21 couldn't be greater – here God shows 'enemies' who he is, not by killing their children, but by his generosity. Enemies still exist, and following Jesus will often make us enemies, but here we begin to see an understanding of God that is about grace and not retribution. So, the long and short of it is that I think the experience of God providing a 'staff' in rough terrain is closer and more immediate than all the green pastures. Just a thought.

Re-engage

The psalm is such a comfort to so many people because it says that trouble will come to an end, and when it's over, God will lead you to place of peace and beauty where you can recover and discover God's presence throughout your trials. For me, the most important application of this psalm is our duty to tell our story. Not only that, but to share it in ways that both glorify God and connect with people.

>Psalm 23 is a perfect example of 'seeker-sensitive' evangelism. It doesn't tell you everything, but it tells you enough to make you curious. And of course it's beautiful, pulling you in like a work of art. It's worth remembering that we are the most beautiful works of art that God has ever made, which means that if we put a little effort into telling our story, we can make something beautiful too.

>Jesus often told stories about God that didn't give all the answers and left people wanting more. How would you tell the story of your relationship with God in this style? Could you write a poem or song, or maybe a story? You may not be confident in showing it to anyone else, but it would be a great way of letting God know how thankful you are for what he's done in your life.

Airlock: Continuing

Where are you right now? In the very dark valley or in the green pastures? Or maybe you're just watching from the sidelines… How can Psalm 23 help you find God today? Why not try rewriting it in modern language. If you were to replace the image of God as a shepherd with something more up to date, what image would you choose? Why?

When it's finished, share it with someone. Pin it up somewhere you can see it every day.

Extra_1 Psalm 100
Extra_2 Matthew 5:1–12

Who's in charge?

C/61

Decompress

Dear Lord, where are you in the world? I see hatred, lies and violence all around. Where are you Lord?

Now read Isaiah 10:5-19

Immerse

Conspiracy theories are very popular at the moment, with topics of supposed cover up involving things like whether an alien spacecraft landed at Roswell way back when, or who actually assassinated of John F Kennedy (if it wasn't Lee Harvey Oswald). Well, here we have the mother of all conspiracies – this one goes right to the top. It is often said when a conspiracy gets as big as this it becomes impossible to fight against.

>The king of Assyria didn't know that he was being used by a greater power. His pride stopped him from seeing that what he was doing was because God had allowed it. Do we rely on God for what we do, or does our pride stop us from sending our thanks right to the top?

Re-engage

Take a look at a newspaper or a news website. Look at the international section, and see what is going on in the world. Where all the trouble spots? Who is fighting whom? Which events does it look like God is nowhere to be seen in?

>Do you believe that God is in control of all those events? Spend some time praying for the events you read about; that God's will will be done! Cut out the stories which you prayed for, and stick them on to a sheet of blank paper. Put this paper up where you'll see it every day. Refresh the stories every week by cutting up up-to-date newspapers and sticking new stories up, and then praying for them whenever you see it.

>Now get hold of a local newspaper and do the same, praying for stories where people or communities are hurting and it looks like God is absent. Is there anything you could do physically to help out the local situations?

>Do you think God uses the the nations of the world today to bring about his will?

Airlock: Continuing

Some will survive

C/62

Decompress

Dear Lord, help me to depend on you,
Through the hard times and the good
Help me to follow you always
The way I always should.

Now read Isaiah 10:20–23

Immerse

Reproduction is an amazing thing when you stop to think about it. Not specifically the act itself, but the number of offspring different creatures have.

>I find it fascinating that some animals produce hundreds and thousands of babies. The reason being that for just a tiny number to survive, a huge number need to be created in the first place, because they're so helpless that the vast majority of them either die or are killed for food. This is good for the predators but unfortunate for the little, helpless babies. Fortunately for us, our chances of survival are very good, and being top of the food chain has distinct advantages!

>As we can see in the passage, the people of Israel were numerous but not all of them were devoted to God.

>This passage introduces us to a theme, or concept, which is of importance to our interpretation of several other Bible passages. The concept is that of a 'righteous remnant'. This concept has been used variously to say that not everyone in the church will go to heaven and also that 'All Israel' will go, in Romans 11:25,26.

>Has your country turned away from God and put its faith in something else? How likely is it that God is going to use a mighty nation to bring your own country under its control?

Re-engage

Make a special effort to pray for your political leaders, especially for the important decisions that they have to make. If you don't know who your local MP is, find out and pray specifically for him or her. Also pray for your local councillor or other local government officials.

Airlock: Continuing

I can't take no more!

C/63

Decompress

If you do something wrong, should you be punished? Does it depend on the seriousness of the offence? Or does all wrongdoing deserve some kind of punishment? Think carefully.

Now read Isaiah 24–34

Immerse

One way of looking at the Bible is to think of it as the story of people messing up, making mistakes and turning away from God, and then, through punishment or forgiveness, or a mixture of the two, getting back on track with him. The mistakes generally have consequences though, some more serious than others. In these chapters, the consequence for turning away from God was quite severe; God's people were getting a political kicking.

>Isaiah's prophecy to God's people doesn't give a crass response to the situation. It accepts full responsibility and it offers hope. We still mess up, make mistakes and turn away from God. But there is for us now, as there was for God's people then, a message of hope.

>Whatever the consequences of our actions, God's words here of 'do not be afraid' are echoed later in the New Testament by Jesus and are echoed throughout history to all who follow Christ. Whatever we are going through, God is there with us.

Re-engage

If there is a situation which you are in the middle of at the moment take it to God in prayer, call on him to help and hear his words to you, 'do not be afraid!' Is there anyone you can pray with about the situation? Could you arrange to meet with them regularly?

>Check out Psalm 56:10,11. 'I praise God for his word to me. I praise the Lord for his word. I trust in God. I will not be afraid. What can people do to me?'

>Put the words of verse 11 on to your mobile phone so you see them every time you switch it on. Be encouraged!

Airlock: Continuing

The good old days

C/64

Decompress

'Lord, be with me as I look at your word. Help me take time out from the pressures and pain of today.'

Now read Isaiah 11:1-11

Immerse

We often long for the good old days, wishing that we could go back to the days when everything was alright, that we could escape the present with all its problems and return to a time when everything was wonderful, children respected their parents and the streets were paved with gold. Unfortunately that isn't possible – what has happened has happened and we can't turn back time. And even if we could, we'd probably find the good old days had their problems and bad points just like today.

>Isaiah's prophecy deals with the messy present by looking to the future, but it does so by building on what has happened and what was great in the past. This passage talks about the coming Messiah, God's chosen one, Jesus.

Re-engage

It's very easy to get bogged down in what has gone before and never look forward. Our story is very important though. Just like God's people could look back fondly and remember the good things that God had done, and then use those memories as the springboard for the future, so can we.

>If you are dealing with some 'mess' in your current situation look back to times when you were close to God. Remember the spiritual highs you've had, and how you felt at those times. Then look forward to the future; it's the same God who was with you then who is with you now and who will be in the future.

>Write a song, or a poem about your walk with Jesus. Look back at the things that have happened in the past and recall them in verse. Likewise look at where you are now and finally put your hopes and dreams of the future into your poem, asking God to be with you and guide you.

Airlock: Continuing

Reunion

Decompress

'Lord, you have done wonderful things in the past
Let me say thank you and long may they last
But as I move forward, let me look up and not down
Prepare the way for me, clear the waters, and don't let me drown.'

Now read Isaiah 11:12–16

Immerse

Manchester United won the European Cup in 1999, where they scored two goals in the dying minutes to win the match. Since that game, whenever watching Manchester United play there is always the feeling, for me anyway, that they can win a match, from whatever position they are in. That expectation has made the games more interesting for me, but at the same time it often leaves me disappointed when they don't turn the result around and win. However, I still have that expectation that anything could happen.

>Because of what God had done at the time of the Exodus, the people of Judah understood Isaiah's words and would now live in expectation of what was to come.

Re-engage

How often do you sit down in prayer and give God a long list of what you would like him to do. One thing about these passages in Isaiah is that they show us that God is in control. If that is the case, should our prayers be more about, 'your will be done' instead of, 'Dear Lord, I just want to ask if you could...'?

>Try praying without asking God to do anything for yourself, others or any situation. Restrict your prayer to just praising God for what he has done and what he will do in the future – just for today

>Do you think this prophecy about Israel and Judah was fulfilled when the Exiles returned from Assyria and Babylon, or do you think it is still being fulfilled today? How would this affect our view on events in the Middle East?

Airlock: Continuing

Because of our focus on the
'forgiving' Jesus do we forget about
the 'angry' God? Why?

Extra_1 Chronicles 36:15–21
Extra_2 Psalm 103:8